D0484278

The Coming
Currency Collapse

OTHER BOOKS BY JEROME F. SMITH

Silver Profits in the Seventies
(1971) ERC Publishing Company

Understanding Runaway Inflation
(1973) ERC Publishing Company

The Reinstitution of Money
(1978) ERC Publishing Company

The Coming Currency Collapse

and what you can do about it

Jerome F. Smith

BOOKS IN FOCUS  NEW YORK

Copyright © 1980 by Jerome F. Smith

All rights reserved. No portion of this book may be reproduced or transmitted in any form, mechanical or electronic, without written permission from Books In Focus, Inc., except by a reviewer who may quote brief passages in connection with a review.

Manufactured in the United States of America

Library of Congress catalog card number: 80-66758

ISBN: 0-916728-41-2

Books In Focus, Inc.
P.O. Box 3481
Grand Central Station
New York, New York 10163
(212) 490-0334

OUR PUBLISHING PHILOSOPHY

BOOKS IN FOCUS is dedicated to publishing Works which lead mankind to Freedom, Justice, and Enlightenment. We shall present books which focus on areas of vital human concern; which accurately identify problems and solutions in these areas; and which identify positive goals toward which rational men and women can move. Your support and suggestions in this are always welcome and appreciated.

Stephen A. Zarlenga
Publisher

TO
Henry David Thoreau
and
kindred noble spirits
everywhere

Foreword

The decade of the 70s and the current year have seen a growing number of investment advisors, and their newsletters and books, recommending the holding of gold, silver and Swiss francs as "hedges against inflation." Even the establishment economist, Paul Samuelson, recently suggested that gold, while still "that barbaric metal," deserves a place in any sane investor's portfolio during these inflationary times.

Early in 1967, nearly fourteen years ago, a man called Jerome Smith advised his clients to purchase silver at $1.29 per ounce. In 1969, he recommended gold at $44/ounce. He also suggested using a Swiss bank for the holding of such purchases — and forecast the rise of the Swiss franc, which has since more than tripled in value in U.S. dollar terms. Those people who followed Smith's advice more than ten years ago have multiplied their assets ten times or more.

In retrospect, of course, it is easy for any investment advisor to "create" a track record by selectively quoting only those recommendations which made a profit, and by ignoring those which didn't turn out too well. For Jerome Smith, that's a difficult procedure to follow, since *all* his investment recommendations have turned out to be profitable — a record that no one else in the business can emulate — while many have passed on his investment advice as their own.

The reason for Smith's success is simple to explain, though it may be a little more difficult for most to follow. Jerome Smith is an economist — and before you put this book back on the shelf realize that Smith is one of a handful of economists whose livelihood depends on being right. He analyzes the past, present and future, not on some government grant or for some government agency, but for individuals like you and me who pay a price for his advice.

Neither you nor I are interested in economic forecasting unless we can *profit* from it. Not one of Jerome Smith's thousands of longstanding clients would have paid his annual fee more than once — unless they had profited from his advice.

But as I said, Smith is one of those few people who make their living from being consistently right about the future and the reason Smith is so often correct stems from his grounding in "Austrian" (free market) economics and, therefore, his understanding of the effects of government actions on the future value of tangible assets.

This is Jerome Smith's fourth book, though it's the first to be made available to the general public. His *Silver Profits in the Seventies*, published in 1971, remains in my opinion, the best example of economic analysis ever written. It shows why the price of silver had to rise from $1.29 per ounce — and why it must still rise from current levels. His *Understanding Runaway Inflation* (1973) shows why the rates of inflation we have seen to date are just the opening round to a German-style inflation yet to come. And his *Reinstitution of Money* (1978) will be recognized in the near future as a classic contribution to economic theory in the heritage of Adam Smith, Ricardo and Ludwig von Mises.

Yet, these three works were but a prelude to *The Coming Currency Collapse — and What You Can Do About It*. This volume represents the fruition of more than fourteen years of economic, monetary and investment research. It shows a sane and conservative path to asset stability in the immediate and not-too-distant future. More importantly, you can learn how to protect yourself and your family from the inevitable progression of "double-digit" inflation to "triple-digit" inflation and more.

Jerome Smith did not cash in his chips in the 1970s after his three very successful recommendations. In addition to advising on other forms of holding gold and silver, such as numismatic coins and gold stocks, his research led him to recommend platinum at $150 in August 1977, just a month before its price began an upward move which didn't stop until it was over $1,000 an ounce. A year later, he recommended diamonds, which have since risen more than 50 percent in dollar terms.

Many investment advisors and newsletter publishers current-ly in business owe their start to Jerome Smith. I am proud to be one of those people. This book enables you to receive, first-hand, the wisdom of a man who has made more money for his clients in the past decade than anyone else in the business. Savor this book. Learn from it, and understand. And follow Jerome Smith's recommendations. If his perceptions of the 1980s are as keen as they were early in the 1970s, as I am convinced they will be, ten years from now you'll be very happy, and a lot richer.

—Mark Tier, Editor
World Money Analyst

Acknowledgments

In attempting to produce this book, which involves some rather complex subjects, in a manner suited to both the general reader and the more informed professional, I am indebted to many people. First of all, I owe a debt to the late Ludwig von Mises for most of my understanding of the underlying principles of human action involved herein; and also to several other laissez-faire Austrian school economists, most of whom were his students, and especially to Dr. Murray Rothbard and Dr. F.A. Hayek. I am also indebted to Christopher P. Weber for reviewing the manuscript, to Helen Yeomans for editing it, to Stephen Zarlenga for encouragement, to Alexander Chin for his illustrations, and last but not least, to my wife Barbara, who typed the manuscript and cracked the whip.

Contents

Introduction

The Gods see what is to come, wise men see what is coming,
ordinary men see what is come.
— Appolonius

One of the most remarkable aspects of human behavior is
the lack of thought and care most otherwise intelligent people
give to investment decisions concerning their personal savings.
Largely this probably reflects their concentration on their own
particular professional concerns to the relative exclusion of
most other things. But much of this also, I believe, is due to the
lack of understanding of the vital nature, character, function
and purpose of savings.

Conceptually, at the individual level, savings can be looked
upon as the accumulation of the surplus of one's productive efforts. When an individual provides a service and voluntarily
exchanges it for payment received, that payment represents a
use of part of his life that is forever lost through the act of providing the service. Life's effort, a passing thing, is traded for a
medium of exchange which, when sound, is durable in value
and can be used at *some future time.*

In normal times, with sound money that holds its value, the
savers and investors, i.e., the capitalists, funnel their surplus
production into the capitalization of industry and commerce,
either directly by share ownership or indirectly through savings with financial intermediaries, and thus they reap the
harvest of a return on their capital.

In the two decades following World War II, when most
people now looking toward retirement were maturing, all the
traditional rules for investing worked well. If you wanted safety and a moderate but secure return on your investment
capital, you bought some mutual fund shares and put some of
your dollars on deposit or bought bonds to earn interest, and

you bought cash-value life insurance both to secure the financial future of your loved ones and to build up a nest egg through self-imposed forced savings. If you were the fortunate recipient of an inheritance or other windfall, you bought an annuity, for the same reasons. Only then, after these basics had been provided, did you venture to seek higher but riskier returns and/or capital gains in land, rental units, venture capital formations, common stocks, etc. And, for most investors, speculations such as commodities or collectibles were not only avoided but totally ignored. All of the traditional rules and practices worked very well for two decades. . . *but they haven't worked in the past decade.*

In inflationary times, new paper money is created, in effect, out of nothing. When the rate of saving and the rate of monetary inflation are about even — such as they were in the decade of the 1960s, the surplus production, i.e., the newly created capital, is drained away by the thefts of this inflation. Of course the drain on capital affects various industries and companies in different ways and degrees so that some are still able to grow and to operate profitably.

As inflation accelerates and exceeds the rate of saving by an increasing margin (as happened during the 1970s), fewer and fewer industries are able to obtain capital to grow and continue to operate profitably. Then, a point is reached (the late 1970s) where most companies' and industries' losses generally, in real terms, exceed diminishing profits, and a further point is reached (1979) where money on deposit depreciates in purchasing value faster than it earns interest income.

Recognition of these realities is now hitting corporate managers, corporate shareholders, professional money managers and even savings account holders and investors generally. Unfortunately most of them, novices and professionals alike, lack knowledge of either monetary history or economic science. Thus, they do not understand what's happening, where it will lead, or what to do about it.

The roots of the world's paper money problems today — and the potential for a stratospheric explosion in the gold price — date from the World War I era. In 1913, the U.S. instituted both the income tax and the Federal Reserve central bank, paving the way, in principle, for unlimited taxation and unlimited deficit spending and paper money creation, as the means of financing an unpopular world war. The only impediment, the gold standard, was suspended during World War I by all participating nations.

Following the inflationary paper money issues of World War I, there was the usual deflation (1920-21) and short recession (1921-22). Instead of returning to the gold standard, as nations had done following the wars in the preceding century, the major nations' central bankers agreed to abandon permanently two essential stabilizing features of the gold standard, retaining only the unstable shell as an operating international monetary system.

The first essential feature abandoned was the former requirement that *only gold* could be counted as a monetary reserve asset; the second was that *only gold* could be used to settle residual international account balances. The international monetary agreements of the early 1920s for the first time provided that a nation *could also count its holdings of redeemable foreign currencies* (particularly the English pound and the U.S. dollar) and credits in such currencies *as monetary reserve assets* on an equal footing with gold itself, and that such currencies could be used in international payments in place of gold. Paper gold was "invented."

The political big spenders were quick to take advantage of their new spending power. Government spending and the paper money supply all grew at unprecedented rates for peacetime in the 1920s. The monetary bubble burst in 1929 and led to the Great Depression of the 1930s. Legally, people could still turn in their paper money and demand gold in most countries — and they did, for a time. This particular remnant of the "gold standard" system had not yet been discarded. The Gold Reserve Act of 1934 eliminated this third essential feature of the gold standard; it terminated circulation of gold coins and free convertibility of paper currency into gold for U.S. residents, and prohibited U.S. citizens from holding gold in the United States (a prohibition that Eisenhower in the 1950s extended to holding gold abroad).

Again in World War II, international redeemability of currencies was suspended — and many currencies were hyperinflated to destruction. Following World War II and the (in)famous Bretton Woods conference, all nations except the U.S. permanently abandoned gold redeemability of their currencies. The U.S. dollar resumed redeemability internationally and, one by one over a period of years, most other national currencies became convertible into dollars. Throughout the 1950s and early 1960s the dollar remained freely and readily redeemable to foreign official institutions.

Internationally, until 1968, the dollar remained legally a promise to pay 1/35 of an ounce of gold to foreign official holders on demand and, in effect, to private parties through the London market whenever the price rose more than a little over the $35 official price. In actual practice, the legal commitment was merely a political promise and was quite meaningless when the chips were down. In March of 1968, the U.S. and other members of the IMF (which included all of the monetarily important trading nations, except Switzerland) put an embargo on gold payments to private parties through sales in the London market, while reasserting that transfers would continue to be made between central banks and governments at $35 per ounce (though very few such transfers were actually made after that time). This act, in fact, amounted to a declaration of the bankruptcy of the dollar, the IMF, the international monetary system, and all the individual currencies of IMF member countries. From that point on there has been no legal or procedural restraint of any kind, domestically or internationally, on the unlimited printing and spending of paper dollars by the U.S. government — nor on the paper money printing and spending of any other government that accepts paper dollars as "reserve assets."

Under a full gold standard, with honest banking, the *money supply is fixed*, excepting inconsequential, tiny amounts (less than 1 percent annually of existing supplies) periodically added by mining. *Widespread inflation is impossible*.

Under a partial gold standard, with fractional-reserve banking, the *money supply is expandable within known but arbitrary limits* which, at any given time, are determined by legally decreed reserve ratios. *Inflation is institutionalized and unavoidable*.

Under a fiat paper "money" system, also with fractional-reserve banking, manipulated by the government's central bank, the *money supply is expandable without limit at the whim of the spendthrift state.* Over a period of time, the rate of depreciation of the fiat unit inevitably exceeds the rate of currency inflation and leads eventually to the currency unit becoming worthless.

In today's advanced stage of high double-digit inflation, prices go up faster than incomes; dollars available for living expenses buy less and less even while nominal dollar incomes (and income taxes) rise. Savings in banks, savings and loan companies, credit unions, in insurance policies and in other fixed-amount forms lose principal value faster than they earn interest income. Most people, with dollar incomes and dollar savings that don't keep pace, are suffering a decline in their actual standard of living and face the prospect of retirement in poverty.

What can one do to escape the plight of most people, cope effectively with today's inflation and prudently provide for the future? It is the task of this book to provide some insights and answers to these questions.

The Coming
Currency Collapse

Before

1913

After

CHAPTER ONE

Background to the Dollar Crisis

Through the centuries, two commodities, *gold* and *silver*, have emerged as money in the free competition of the market. . . .If paper notes or bank deposits are used as money substitutes . . . [they] are simply warehouse receipts for actually deposited gold . . . as a convenient stand-in for gold, not as an increment.
—Murray N. Rothbard
What Has Government Done to Our Money?

Article I, Section 8 of the Constitution authorizes Congress (the federal government): "to coin money and regulate the value thereof." The verb "to coin" means to make metal into coins by stamping. As it is impossible to regulate value, the only sensible interpretation of the founders' intent on this point is that they meant Congress could "regulate the denominations thereof" domestically and, perhaps, *thereby* establish parity rates with foreign coins based on the relative weights and purities.

Article I, Section 10, says: "No state shall. . .coin money; emit bills of credit; make anything but gold and silver coin a tender in payment of debts" (i.e., money). Clearly, the Constitution only authorizes the federal government to coin gold and silver coins, and prohibits the states from doing so while *explicitly obliging them to exclude anything else from any legal standing as money.*

Before 1913

Gold and silver coins, coined by the U.S. mint in accordance with the U.S. Constitution, were the principal money used in the U.S. for over 140 years. Paper money, whether it

3

was banknotes issued by state-chartered banks or gold or silver certificates issued by the federal treasury, was redeemable in the gold or silver coin it represented. Everyone knew that banknotes and certificates were not money but were simply convenient money substitutes. Excepting the Civil War greenbacks, paper money generally was backed by the coin deposited for which the receipt (i.e., banknote or certificate) was issued. Our money was honest; in a word, paper money was sound.

Throughout most of the last century, money issuers generally undertook to redeem their paper money for the metal on demand. Under this system there is a built-in restraint on each issuer of money not to issue more paper money than he is able to redeem if called upon to do so. For this reason, inflation was not a major problem in the last century; though there were isolated and shortlived examples here and there, it was certainly not a widespread problem. And, in any individual locality, if an issuer of paper money did issue excessive amounts, he was quickly brought into line by people calling for redemption.

The system also worked with integrity and non-inflationary efficiency internationally in world trade. For a full century, until 1913, the United States, Great Britain and most other nations were either on a bi-metallic gold and silver system or were on the full gold standard. The pound, the dollar and most other currencies were each defined as specific weights of gold and the resulting official price of gold was fixed by statute. Banknotes and national currencies were fully redeemable in gold, and gold was freely exported and imported to settle international accounts.

This made it automatic that international trade and/or payments imbalances (deficits or surpluses) *could not occur*, and that general price levels in the various participating nations *could not vary* from one nation to another by any more than the cost of shipment of gold. This system also made it impossible for "monetary managers" to inflate or deflate the money supply of either the national or global economy.

In general, states historically have taxed to obtain their revenues. They resort to printing press inflation to "finance"

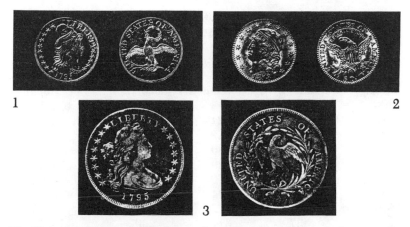

1   2

3

The United States originally adopted a bi-metallic standard of coinage because of the scarcity of both gold and silver and the popularity of silver coins. Shown here are obverse and reverse of (1) the first type of gold half eagle (1795), (2) an 1818 gold half eagle, and (3) a 1795 silver dollar. (Courtesy of the American Numismatic Society, New York.)

spending in excess of their tax revenues. We are accustomed in this century to levels of taxation and state spending that have never existed before in history. To illustrate that point let's review briefly the record of the history of taxation in the United States; for tax rates and inflation rates are inextricably intertwined.

Today it is hard to imagine that in 1800 the total tax revenue of the United States government was the "enormous" sum of $13 million and total federal spending was $10 million — they were running a surplus. That was a good start for a new nation. On a per person basis, had you been around in those times you would have paid the enormous sum per annum of $2.17 to support your federal government. In the decade of 1810, which encompassed the critical war of 1812, spending more than doubled, to $24 million , with revenues at $21 million, reenacting a historical pattern of a state incurring a deficit to support a war. On a per person basis the level of taxation increased to $2.63 a year.

In the decades of the 1820s and 1830s normalcy returned, taxes stabilized around a total revenue figure of $26 million and spending around $20 million, representing taxes of $2.00 a head. In the 1840s with the advent of the Mexican War,

TABLE I

100 Years of Growth — U.S. Population and Federal Finances

Decade Starting	Average Population (millions)	Federal Annual Average Receipts (millions of dollars)	Spending	Federal Receipts per Capita
1800	6	13	10	$ 2.17
1810	8	21	24a	2.63
1820	11	22	16	2.00
1830	15	30	24	2.00
1840	20	29	34b	1.45
1850	27	60c		2.22
1860	36	304	504d	8.44
1870	45	312	271	6.93
1880	37	371	269	10.00
1890	70	394	410e	5.63
100-Year Increase:	x11	x30	x41	x2

a. Increase associated with the War of 1812.
b. Increase associated with the Mexican War.
c. Doubling of federal tariffs and spending led to Civil War.
d. Eightfold jump to wage Civil War.
e. Increase associated with the Spanish War.

spending jumped nearly 50 percent and the nation again went into the red.

By the 1850s things had gotten out of hand. Total tax revenues (without a war) doubled in that decade alone. Mostly these were tariffs benefiting northern manufacturers, and they led to resentment in the South and ultimately to the Civil War. That's when things really took off. In the 1850s total tax revenues of the federal government were around $60 million and total spending was around the same figure.

In the decade of the 1860s they jumped by many times to revenues around $300 million and spending of $500 million. This is the average for that decade. It jumped the per person taxation from $2.22 in the 1850s to over $8, almost a fourfold increase, in the 1860s. And that's when the United States republic sank below the surface of reality — for it ceased to exist.

It was during this period of time, actually beginning in the 1840s (during the time of the Mexican War) that Henry David Thoreau wrote his famous essays. A notable thought from one of those essays was: "I heartily accept the motto — 'That government is best which governs least;' . . . Carried out, it finally amounts to this, which I also believe — 'That government is best which governs not at all;' and when men are prepared for it, that will be the kind of government which they will have." This, in the words of the Declaration of Independence, is a standard to which the wise and the just can repair.

After the Civil War things came back down. Conservative fiscal and taxation policies were resumed, but at the new high plateau. The greenbacks which had been issued in profusion to finance the federal government's attack on the South were gradually retired and by 1878 they were reestablished at a parity with redeemable currency. The following three decades were the most prosperous period in the history of any nation anywhere, with balanced federal budgets and/or surpluses in most years, no inflation, and a declining price level.

Taxes stabilized around $300 to $400 million per annum in the last quarter of the 19th century. This continued until the decade of 1910 which encompassed the World War I period and again, as had happened in the Civil War period, nation-states resorted to printing press inflation to finance their wars. But for the entire century preceding, federal revenues (mostly from import tariffs) averaged only $162 million annually — less than $5 per person! If the U.S. federal apparatus today were operated in the same fashion, taking into account that today's dollar is worth about 1/7th what it averaged then and that today's population is about eight times larger than the 19th century average, the U.S. federal budget would be balanced at a mere $9 billion ($40 per person)! Instead of this, U.S. federal spending today is more than 50 times these figures, the federal state looms 50 times more powerful in relation to each individual, and we therefore have two percent as much freedom as our grandparents had!

The century from 1814 to 1913 was the period of the soundest nationally-issued currencies that ever existed in history — before or since. All national currencies were tied to precious metals. In Europe and the Americas it was a bimetallic standard, with silver predominating in the early part of that period and subsequently declining in monetary importance (because it became more available in quantity) while gold became relatively more scarce and more important; but all currencies were tied to one or the other or both of these precious metals and were redeemable.

Overall there was no depreciation of money. Short bursts of inflation occurred within particular countries, usually associated with one war or another. But taking the century as a whole, prices were at about the same level in 1913 as they were in 1814.

After 1913

Beginning with 1913, in the United States in particular, two entirely different concepts came to the fore and resulted subsequently in the destruction of the soundness of official paper money. The two different concepts I am referring to are the Federal Reserve System and the Income Tax. The Federal Reserve System came in, in the United States, through legislation that was introduced on December 23 just as the Congressmen were preparing to go home for the holiday. It was passed, not because anyone understood what they were voting on or had examined it carefully, but simply because they wanted to go home for Christmas. During that same year, the Constitutional Amendment to establish the Income Tax was voted in, by default; mostly people accepted it and brought it in through Constitutional Amendment process on the basis of the assurances of the promoters that the tax rate would never go over one percent of most people's income, so why worry about it?

Those two political changes laid the cornerstones for the rise of the warfare/welfare state and for the destruction of the soundness of the United States currency.

In the present century, so far at least, population, technology, production and government have grown at highly disparate rates.

During and after World War I the United States and Great Britain, while still paying lip-service to the gold standard, abandoned its restraints and printed unbacked inflationary

TABLE II

80 Years of Growth   —   U.S. Population and Federal Finances

Decade Starting	Population (millions)	Federal Annual Average Receipts (million of dollars)	Spending (million of dollars)	Federal Receipts per Capita
1900	76	594	587	7.82
1910	92	1,495	3,821f	16.25
1920	106	4,438	3,677	41.87
1930	123	3,769	6,141g	30.64
1940	132	29,364	50,130h	222.45
1950	151	61,505	64,983i	407.32
1960	179	110,372	114,641j	616.60
1970	203	380,980	415,500	1,876.75
1980s (projected)	222	1,200,000	1,500,000	5,405.00
80-Year Increase (to start-1980):	x3	x960	x1022	x332

f. Sixfold jump to fund WWI.
g. New Deal doubling.
h. Eightfold jump to fund WWII.
i. Increase associated with Korean War.
j. Doubling of federal revenues and spending associated with Vietnam War.

paper money to finance the war. As a result, prices generally doubled — except for the gold price, which was officially fixed. Because of this disparity, the production of gold following World War I decreased at a time when more gold was needed at official parity rates to support the inflated paper money supplies. The obvious and correct solution, deflation of the bloated paper money supplies (and thereby the price and wage levels), was politically unpopular and the relative shortage of gold meant that a return to the full gold standard was impossible. The subsequent steps down the road from fully redeemable currencies to today's fiat money and global inflation, are set forth briefly below.

1922   Adoption of the gold exchange standard. To "economize on the monetary uses of gold" the pound and the dollar were officially declared "as good as gold"; these currencies were deemed fit to be used along with gold in the monetary "reserves" of other countries.

1933-37   The domestic redeemability of U.S. and other national currencies in gold was officially revoked and competitive devaluations reduced the international gold value of currencies.

1939-45   Extreme monetary inflations in Europe in World War II destroyed most European currencies and forced most continentals to resort to barter at the close of World War II.

1944   Bretton Woods Agreement. Creation of the International Monetary Fund (IMF) and agreement to fix all exchange rates in terms of the dollar and the dollar in terms of gold; thus, the dollar became the principal reserve currency and the only currency any longer directly redeemable in gold internationally. The stage was set for global dollar inflation.

1958   Following years of gradually increasing inflation, U.S. dollars held abroad now exceeded U.S. gold reserves. Perceiving this, certain countries (notably France) began calling for gold in exchange for their dollar reserves.

1961   Officials began to be alarmed at the amount of gold leaving the U.S. Treasury. Evidence of the concern of individuals and institutions about the ability of the U.S. to continue honoring its promise to pay gold surfaced when the private market price of gold rose well above the official price. To counter this, the U.S. and nine other major nations formed the London Gold Pool, agreeing to support the dollar in the London gold market by selling gold for dollars when the price rose above the official rate of $35/oz.

1965   The U.S. abandoned silver. Thirty years of paper money inflation and price escalation caused the face amount of silver coins to fall below the store-of-value worth of the silver metal they contain. Hence, they were withdrawn from circulation, first, by value-conscious individuals and, later, after official minting of base metal replacement coinage, massively by the U.S. Treasury. (Essentially the same thing, for the same reasons, is happening to copper pennies in the 1980s.)

1968   Currency crises and devaluations, and growing world market demand for gold and silver (with pressures for upward changes in the official price of gold), were recurring phenomena of the 1960s. Persistent and accelerating U.S. monetary inflation had put too great a pressure on the gold price; by early 1968, other gold pool members no longer dared continue selling gold for questionable paper dollars. The crisis in early 1968 culminated in March with the end of the London Gold Pool. The United States had supplied more than half the gold offered by the pool in its stabilization efforts. During a decade when the United States was running large balance-of-payments deficits and refused to deflate, it was obvious that continuation of this policy would result in complete depletion of the United States' monetary gold stock. When it became apparent that such a situation would result in utter chaos in the international monetary system, the "pool" device was abandoned and the central bankers boycotted the gold market in London and elsewhere, blandly announcing that they expected the market price of gold (now to be determined by private demand) would fall below the official price. It didn't; it rose.

Further, in 1968 Congress eliminated the requirement that the Federal Reserve hold gold certificates equal to at least 25 percent of the value of Federal Reserve notes. This removed the last tenuous domestic connection between the dollar and gold.

1971   The free market price of gold continued to rise well beyond the official international dollar redemption price. Central banks could no longer be stalled in their redemption demands by the U.S. government; their demands for U.S. monetary gold became insistent and in August President Nixon reacted by declaring that the dollar would no longer be redeemable in gold. Gold moved to new highs in the free private gold market.

1972-74   Double-digit inflation in the U.S. The price of gold soared. Central banks attempted to maintain the official fixed exchange rates between currencies set at Bretton Woods, which meant buying up still more dollars flooding the market — which meant in turn printing more of their own currencies; accelerating U.S. monetary inflation was thus exported globally.

1973   On February 13, 1973, the United States announced another devaluation of the dollar, from $38 per ounce to $42.22 per ounce of gold. This became legally effective on September 21, 1973. However, no official gold transactions were ever effected at the official "price" of $42.22 per ounce.

First the Swiss then other central banks refused to support fixed exchange rates against an unending and increasing flood of dollars; the dollar tumbled in value against the German mark, the yen, the Swiss franc and other currencies.

Floating exchange rates resulted and were subsequently officially agreed to, which meant letting the foreign-exchange markets determine the rate for each currency. Because of the continuing flood of dollars this evolved into the "dirty float": central banks purchased dollars as they deemed necessary to try to keep their own rates stable; in theory they could also sell dollars when necessary — except that it is never necessary, because of ongoing runaway deficit spending and debt monetization in the U.S.

What we have seen since is all the unavoidable consequences of "floating" (i.e., anchorless) currencies and everything that preceded this occurrence. We now have a world in which there are absolutely *no* restraints whatsoever on the United States *or any other state* on printing paper money units. Either physically printing them or putting them in the central bank computers by simply making an entry. There are no restraints domestically; there are none internationally.

1974   April—The finance ministers of the EEC (European Economic Community) conferred about gold. They agreed to permit central banks to settle accounts among themselves in gold at market-related prices. To date no officially reported gold transactions have occurred.

June—The Group of Ten decided to permit gold (at market-related prices) to be used as collateral for loans between official institutions. Two months later, Italy collateralized some of its official gold in a borrowing of $2 billion from Germany secured by about 16.5 million ounces of gold (at a collateral value of about $120 per ounce).

1975   November—The heads of government of West Germany, Italy, Japan, France, Canada, the United Kingdom, and the United States met in Rambouillet, France to discuss the international monetary situation. Agreement was reached for more official intervention in the foreign-exchange markets in order to reduce fluctuations in exchange rates, and a first draft of Article IV (Obligations Regarding Exchange Agreements) of the revised IMF Articles of Agreement was proposed.

1976   January — The Interim Committee of the IMF met in Kingston, Jamaica at which time it presented the revised Articles of Agreement of the

Fund. Most of the agreements reached were re-statements of proposals made by the IMF Monetary Negotiations Committee in September 1975, including (1) the ending of an "official" price for gold, (2) the selling of about 25 million ounces of gold held by the IMF, and (3) the restitution of about 25 million ounces of gold to the member nations. Also agreed upon were increases in the IMF quotas (and likewise in the lines of credit from which the member nations can borrow) by 33.5 percent, and the permission for member nations to adopt either fixed or floating exchange rates. Member nations were *not permitted* to fix the value of their currencies to gold, however.

June — The heads of government of West Germany, Japan, France, Italy, Canada, the United Kingdom, and the United States met in Puerto Rico to continue discussions begun at Rambouillet concerning the international monetary situation. The most urgent problem appeared to be what to do about the disorder in the foreign-exchange markets. No decisions about this, or any other topic, were announced, however.

1977   January — The Bank for International Settlements (BIS) announced that the United States, Japan, West Germany, Belgium, Canada, Sweden, the Netherlands, and Switzerland had agreed to provide the equivalent of another $3 billion in standby credit to Great Britain, separate from the $3.9 billion loans agreed to by the G-10 countries only two weeks earlier. The stated purpose of both of these loans was to help prevent a further reduction in the monetary reserves of Great Britain, which British officials were using to purchase pounds in the foreign-exchange markets in attempts to bolster the exchange rate of the pound.

January-June — The United States incurred a current-account Balance of Payments (BOP) deficit of a record $8.8 billion during this period. Partly as a result of this, the exchange value of the dollar decreased to new lows in terms of the Swiss franc and German mark.

August — The September 1975 agreement among the G-10 countries that the total stock of gold held by them would not be increased expired. It was agreed that, effective April 1, 1978, these and other nations might add to their gold reserves as they saw fit.

1978   November — In the face of a renewed plunge in the dollar, the U.S. Treasury obtained a massive loan of Japanese yen, Swiss francs and German marks (equivalent to U.S $30 billion), directly from the governments of a group of industrialized nations, to be used in foreign-exchange market interventions in support of the U.S. dollar in late 1978 and in 1979.

Borrowing for Disaster

Throughout the 1970s the U.S., by pressuring the other industrial nations to co-operate, effectively continued to enjoy the Bretton Woods system benefits of sponsoring the principal reserve and trading currency for the world — without being burdened with the redeemability and exchange-rate maintenance responsibilities that were the foundation of that now-defunct system.

As absurd as it patently was, the other industrial nations, especially Germany and Switzerland, actually reinforced the United States' global inflation monopoly with the $30-billion (in foreign funds) rescue package announced in late 1978. They agreed with the U.S., in effect, that "because the U.S. had used its special position irresponsibly in the past and had thereby flooded foreign financial institutions with well over $700 billion of irredeemable fiat dollars, we volunteer to assist the U.S. to do more of the same, while minimizing foreign-exchange market consequences on the dollar, by loaning the

U.S. huge additional amounts of our own currencies on favorable terms."

Thus, in addition to continuing to enjoy the benefits of massive dollar purchases by foreign central banks (in foreign-exchange interventions), the U.S. has itself been able to buy additional massive dollar amounts in foreign-exchange markets. Foreign central bankers (particularly Germany and Switzerland) thus gave U.S. officials a new power, one they naturally expected would be used conservatively but effectively to "defend the dollar."

They thereby reaffirmed their faith in the fiction that the U.S. fiscal and monetary authorities would reform their profligate natures, reverse course, become conservative, and begin honestly, wisely and successfully to administer a fiat reserve currency for the world.

1979   The combination of the change from a long-standing policy of benign neglect to a "strong defense of the dollar," signalled by the Carter administration in November 1978, and the new "tight money" policy repeatedly shouted from the roof-tops throughout 1979 by Federal Reserve Chairman Paul Volcker, stabilized the dollar and the foreign-exchange markets generally in 1979 — compared to 1978, at least. It was a relative calm that bore a high-price, however, much of which is yet to be paid.

Firstly, it was predictable then that the $30 billion of strong currencies borrowed to support the dollar will no doubt quickly be exhausted in the next renewed dollar crisis and must then be rolled over. Excepting the temporary cosmetic effect, no nation can strengthen its finances by borrowing more from its creditors. Within a year or two the effect is the opposite. Secondly, Volcker's "tight money" policy was more talk than action in 1979 and, though presently real, will probably not extend beyond 1980. Nominally high interest rates in the double-digit percentage range are not high when money is depreciating at nearly the same rate — or more.

Further, it is not true that the Fed controls either interest rates or the money supply. The Fed has little choice in the matter of purchasing U.S. Treasury debt issues each week. If the Fed buys less in one week it must buy more the next week — and that is usually the extent of its ability to affect interest rates and money supply expansion, for a week or two at the most. Beyond that limit the Fed does not and cannot *act* in the financial markets, it can only *react* and conform to market forces over any substantial period.

Still further, the relative calm in the foreign-exchange markets in 1979, rather than being any indication of strength in the dollar, was a result of all currencies plunging at about the same pace against the true measure of the worth of paper monies — gold. Gold trebled in dollar price in 1979. This means national currencies generally lost about two-thirds of their value.

Table III gives the tax and inflation percentage record each tenth year, for the U.S. since 1940.

Tax Revolts and Mounting Deficits

TABLE III
U.S. Total Income and Total Taxes
(billions of dollars)

Year	Total Income	Total Taxes	Direct Tax	Inflation*	Total Spending**
1940	$ 78	$ 14	17.9%	2.8%	20.7%
1950	228	55	24.1	7.6	31.7
1960	401	127	31.6	5.3	36.9
1970	804	276	34.3	7.6	41.9
1980 (projected)	2,100	860	41.0	18.0	48.0

*The average annual monetized federal deficit for the preceding ten years as a percent of the current year's total income.
**Not including accumulating unfunded future liabilities.

Several accounts of the burgeoning tax revolt have appeared recently. As long ago as 1973 it was estimated that Washington was losing as much as $30 billion a year in tax revenues. To-day, describing the growing underground economy in the

Chart 1
Total Government Spending

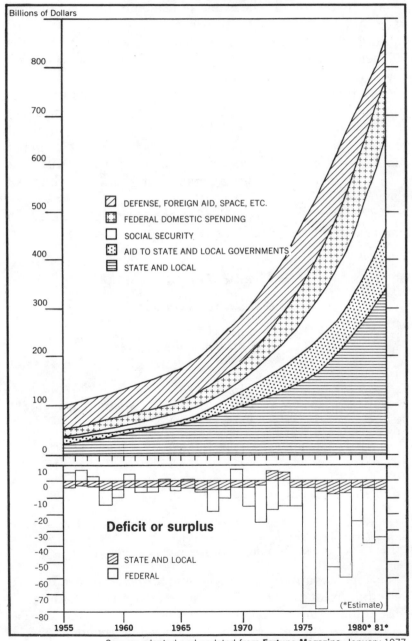

Source: adapted and updated from **Fortune Magazine,** January 1977.

U.S., tax experts estimate that taxpayers failed to pay some $50 billion in 1979 and overdeclared a further $18 billion in deductions.

A Harris Poll conducted eight years ago found that 74 percent of taxpayers "would support a tax revolt." It seems reasonable to assume that today more of those who "would" have joined those who "are." If this is the trend, perhaps there is a connection between the mounting tax revolt and soaring United States federal budget deficits?

The entire course of this century, on a decade-by-decade basis, is characterized by a growth in all official budget and money supply figures on an exponential curve. World War II was the first major war in history that was not followed by a reduction in government budgets by major nations participating in a war. Following World War II the figures just kept growing after a period of only two or three years of restraint in the late 1940s. Chart 1 shows the growth in U.S. federal and state spending from 1955 onwards.

Throughout the 1950s and 1960s federal budget figures grew. As of World War II all the figures had moved up from hundreds of millions to billions. As of the decade of the 1950s revenues averaged $62 billion annually and spending was $65 billion — so that was a decade of deficits on balance in peacetime (excepting the Korean War, which compared to other modern day wars was a small one).

Compared to the 1950s the figures in the 1960s approximately doubled to finance Vietnam warfare and constituent welfare. In the 1960s, we jumped into federal budgets of three-digit billions for the first time with decade-average federal revenues of $110 billion and expenditures of $115 billion. The decade of the 1970s saw a trebling compared to the 1960s. Revenues averaged $380 billion and expenditures averaged nearly $415 billion. Projecting this into the 1980s would indicate average annual federal revenues in excess of $1 trillion and budget deficits averaging $300 billion annually, with most of that being monetized — that can't work. The decade of the 1980s will be the decade of hyperinflation.

Through the ages, gold and silver have been money

CHAPTER TWO

What is Money?

An object cannot be used as money unless, at the moment when its use as money begins, it already possesses an objective exchange-value based on some other use. . . .

— Ludwig von Mises
The Theory of Money and Credit

Money is at once the most important and the most misunderstood economic concept. Its monopolization, perversion and counterfeiting by the state has wrought more havoc and destroyed more life and property than all the armies of history.

For a half-century, most "economists" have been unable to agree even upon a definition of money, much less upon its theoretical nature or on the practical consequences of its use and abuse. Thus, a variety of "professional" opinions have been available on every money question. Among the economic advisors to governments, the most popular and prevalent opinions have been those which cede the most power to the state. And, most often, political decisions based upon these opinions have been the ones most damaging to the populace.

What is money? And what determines what is money? I'm going to take the second question first.

Whatever Markets Select

What is money is determined by the totality of the individual choices of people making exchanges. The first use of money is not directly recorded in history because it occurred much too long ago, prior to recorded history. But we can be certain that it did evolve from a barter system. And it arose spontaneously.

In every society, money was the result of *spontaneous* human action and interaction — not of any preconceived overall plan. The selection of which articles of trade were to be most actively traded over great distances was the spontaneous choice of the exchanges of many individual traders over a period of time.*

Through the centuries, and through the millennia, as a matter of fact, the world society has selected gold and silver as media of exchange. It has selected gold and silver as money. This is the way it is. It is quite useless for anyone — government official, banker, economist, or anyone else — to speculate about what money *should* be. Money is the product of the process of cooperative actions of traders in the markets; if and when something new becomes money it will emerge by the same process.**

In a variety of ways, this *is happening* today. The U.S. nation-state's efforts to demonetize gold have not succeeded in that goal; however, the U.S. and other states have immobilized monetary gold, and by "legal tender" laws, etc., they have deprived domestic and global traders of their right to choose media of exchange that might be more dependable and more convenient than either depreciating national paper or a precious metal. Like life, liberty, property and privacy, sound money, too, is a right. Ultimately modern markets, using modern technology, will determine what money will be in the future. And, with nation-state monopolization and immobilization of global monetary gold, markets may well find something else more available, more convenient and, perhaps, better in other ways.

Money is not a subject upon which governments can legislate effectively. To the degree that various legislative

*How money originated is explained more fully in my book *The Reinstitution of Money* (ERC Publishing Company, 212-585 16th Street, West Vancouver, B.C., Canada, $8.00).

**In 1912, Ludwig von Mises wrote in his *The Theory of Money and Credit* (pp. 69, 71): "The concept of money as a creature of Law and the State is clearly untenable. It is not justified by a single phenomenon of the market. To ascribe to the State the power of dictating the laws of exchange, is to ignore the fundamental problems of money-using society . . . . State declarations of legal tender affect only those monetary obligations that have already been contracted. But commerce is free to choose between retaining its old medium of exchange or creating a new one for itself."

enactments or monarchical decrees or any other pronouncements of governments pertain to money, they have effect only if they are compatible with overall societal decisions about money as expressed in market actions; if they are not compatible, it is only a matter of time until the artificially distorted system breaks down and is replaced by an official or private money unit and system acceptable to markets.

An Economic Good

Money evolved in antiquity. Retrospectively, the classical economists identified three essential characteristics of money: (1) a medium of value in exchange; (2) a standard of value; and lastly, but most importantly (3) a store of value. *Paper money that is not redeemable into something that has a market value apart from its use as money, cannot be a store of value. Paper money that is not a store of value cannot be a standard of value. Such paper money certainly cannot be a medium of value.*

Irredeemable paper is not and cannot be money. It is counterfeit money which appears to be genuine because it looks like a genuine paper money of recent familiarity. Like any other counterfeit money, it can circulate as long as those to whom it is offered *believe* that it is genuine. Once a counterfeit is recognized, it is not accepted in payment; it does not continue to circulate. When people *no longer believe* that it is genuine, it quickly becomes worthless. And, even a long-held false belief, especially one based on an "engineered" deception, can be abandoned with startling suddenness.

Money is the *economic good* (or goods) most widely sought after and offered in *indirect exchanges* for other economic goods and services. An "economic good" is any useful item which is desired and scarce, and therefore valuable. An "indirect exchange" is a two-stage, three-party transaction in which one of the two parties to the first stage of the transaction accepts an economic good in trade which he intends to pay to a third party in the second stage, for another economic good or service that he wants directly for his own use.

Early American Coins

The first coinage in the American Colonies, minted by Massachusetts in 1652.

The Franklin penny of 1787, carrying the motto, "Mind your business."

In the midst of the Civil War, the Secretary of the Treasury was prevailed upon by the Rev. Mr. Watkinson to impose the phrase "In God We Trust" on U.S. coinage. "From my heart I have felt our national shame in disowning God as not the least of our present national disasters," he said.

The good used in payment is thus a means to an end, a tool, a *capital* good. Silver and gold emerged in antiquity as money not only because they were convenient but, more importantly, because they were valued for beauty, utility and durability — their capital service — *over time,* and over great distances. A piece of paper, a deposit receipt for money or an IOU, may circulate in place of money, as a token of debits and credits, but it cannot replace money as a means of final payment. Paper is not capital. Paper is not money. Historically, gold and silver have been the final means of payment.

Even though gold and silver are disparaged as mere commodities, the important fact is that they are *capital* commodities (capital being defined as anything valued for its utility or service *over time*); it is gold's and silver's capital service that got them elected to the office of money — that they are commodities is beside the point.

A Universal Definition of Money

I would like to offer a concise definition of money that has been demonstrated by history, and by markets. *Money is the most liquid form of capital.* The emphasis is on each of these two words, liquid and capital. Now, it is true that there are substitute moneys and they have varying levels of quality. And these substitute paper moneys are much more convenient than metal (gold or silver) itself. There are two forms of substitute paper moneys: equity money and debt money. In the final analysis, the quality of any debt instrument, a promise to pay, has to take second seat to the quality of equity money, an actual payment.

An equity instrument is a completely unqualified ownership document *and* a deposit receipt for the actual money. A debt instrument, on the other hand, has a further element of uncertainty — namely, the financial stability and solvency of the issuer. Any paper money, whether it is issued by a private banker, a goldsmith or a government central bank, is only as good as the integrity of the issuer. The paper is not the money; what is behind it is the actual money.

As discussed above, the classical economists in defining money specified or stipulated, by retrospective study, three separate characteristics of money: (1) it was a store of value; (2) it was a standard of value; and (3) it was a medium of exchange, i.e., a means of *final* payment.

It is worth taking a closer look at these three because they don't match up with the definition I offered, and I would like to highlight the distinction. First of all, we have known for about a century within the field of economics, and psychology as well, that value is subjective. Therefore, we have to distinguish between two different kinds of value when we talk about the store-of-value function of money. One cannot transfer a subjective value. What is actually stored and subject to transfer is the market value and that is derived from, but independent of, the individual subjective values. Because of the subjective nature of value, you cannot have an objective standard of an individual's subjective value. What you can have is a standard of *market* value (which is an approximation of the average of the subjective valuations of all of the individual market participants).

Capital goods fulfill both of these requirements and can therefore emerge (and, by retrospective analysis, have in the past emerged) as money. Capital goods represented by some sort of certificate — shares perhaps (which are simply a secondary form of the primary money that is the ownership itself), bear all the characteristics that are required for money except one, and that is that the market has not yet "adopted" them, so to speak. They have not emerged as money. Gold itself is a capital good, silver is a capital good. They are valued for their services over time. In any event, the economic good most widely sought after and offered in indirect exchange — whatever it is specifically — will emerge as money.

The misuse of double-entry bookkeeping

CHAPTER THREE

The Cause of Inflation

> Money is the greatest invention of all time for economic better-
> ment. It began as private property for purposes of exchange. But
> with passing time and the rise of states, the state control of
> money developed as a means of gaining and holding authoritar-
> ian power. . . .
>
> "Coin clipping" by the state, in whatever form and by what-
> ever name, has been a traditional method by which the state
> exerts and extends power over its subjects.
>
> —Dr. F.A. Harper
> "Introduction," *Inflation and Price Control*

In order to understand inflation and runaway inflation one
must begin with a clear definition of inflation. The common
usage of the word today usually refers to the depreciation of
money (evidenced by generally rising prices), but sometimes
refers to increases in the money supply. It's confusing. Most
often, when the word is used in general circulation publications it is difficult, even in context, to perceive which meaning
the writer intends — quite often the writer himself doesn't
know the distinction. Largely for this reason, most popular articles on the cause(s) of inflation ramble on and on listing a
half dozen or a dozen "causes of inflation," all of which are actually effects of inflation, without ever getting to the underlying cause.

For the purposes of this discussion, I will use the
economically, etymologically, logically and historically correct definition of inflation: *Inflation is any increase of the
money supply*. With this definition it is easy to identify the
cause of inflation. Whatever causes the money supply to increase causes inflation. This definition at least starts us on the
right track to the cause.

As we learned in the last chapter, money is chosen by markets, and the moneys which have emerged through the centuries have been gold and silver. It is interesting to note that historically, the only instance in which the increase of physical gold in circulation was sufficient to depreciate significantly the exchange value of the gold already in circulation, was the Spanish gold inflation in 16th century Europe caused by the massive and sustained importations of gold that the Spaniards had systematically plundered from the Americas.

To find the cause of our present-day inflation, we have to examine not the genuine money which once existed, but the origin of the substitute money we have today, once fully redeemable in gold and silver but now redeemable in nothing at all.

Money Substitutes

A money substitute, as the name implies, is simply something that is offered and accepted in place of the money itself. The first money substitutes were coins of slightly less weight and/or purity than that certified by the local ruler. Initially, these circulated side by side with full weight and full purity coins because: (1) the difference in precious metal content was very slight; (2) the official certification of weight and fineness was taken as an assurance of full weight and fineness; (3) the recipient expected that he would be able to pass them on to someone else on a par with full weight and fully fine coins; and finally (and least importantly) (4) the ruler decreed that his coins be accepted on a par with full weight and fully fine coins.

Inflations of ancient monetary systems proceeded in about the following sequence: (1) the introduction of coin names on the face of official coins in the place of the weight and the fineness certification; (2) the decree of a monopoly of issue by the ruler; (3) the calling-in of all circulating coins for reminting and reissue at a lower weight and/or lower fineness (and

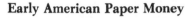

THIS Indented Bill of Twenty
Shillings due from the Massachusets
Colony to the Possessor shall be in value
equal to money & shall be accordingly
accepted by the Treasurer and Receivers
subordinate to him in all Publick paym.ts
and for any Stock at any time in the
Treasury. Boston in New-England
February the third 1690 By Order of
the General Court

Early American Paper Money

The first paper money appeared in 1690 in Massachusetts; a facsimile is shown here. The Colony printed £7,000 of this "money" in varying denominations and used it to pay soldiers who had returned from an unsuccessful expedition against Canada. Even on this small scale, the relationship between paper money and the waging of war is exemplified.

An early example (1790) of New York City debt is shown below.

hence in larger quantity).* This third step would be repeated until the coin became so nearly valueless intrinsically that no one would accept it in exchange, and, after a period of barter and economic stagnation (and not infrequently rebellion), the ruler was forced to reissue precious metal coins to revive trade and industry (and to facilitate his ability to collect taxes).

---

*This, most readers will remember, is precisely what was done to U.S. silver coins in 1965 when they were replaced with base-metal "cupro-nickel" counterfeit coins and silver certificates were first dishonored (1966) and later (1967) withdrawn from circulation.

Paper money substitutes arose in Europe during medieval times. In those days, it was customary for the goldsmiths to serve also as depositories for the safekeeping of gold bullion owned by their wealthy customers. When a customer wanted his gold for a transaction, it was necessary for him to pick it up physically and take it to the party with whom he wanted to exchange, or at least to bring the customer to the goldsmith's shop to witness the transfer of ownership on the goldsmith's record books. With the introduction of the widespread use of paper, however, the practice soon developed that the goldsmith would simply issue a receipt to the depositor, who then had the option later of either presenting the receipt for withdrawal of his gold or, more simply, of merely endorsing the receipt to the person to whom he was making payment. Thus the receipt itself became a money substitute and a means of payment. The recipient then had the same option: he could either turn in the receipt for the gold or endorse it to another recipient.

Before long, for convenience, the goldsmiths began to issue "bearer" receipts, which required no endorsements, and these circulated as easily as gold in transactions; they were of course more convenient. These receipts were the first banknotes.

The Origin of Fractional-Reserve Banking

In issuing these receipts, including small denominations, the goldsmiths (bankers) were clearly in direct competition with the royal coinage monopoly. Royalty, rather than being outraged, was apparently fascinated to observe that the public seemed to prefer the goldsmith's paper to the king's (underweight and impure) metal coins. Also, it was obvious that it was easier successfully to issue counterfeit paper receipts for precious metal that were accepted as genuine, than it was to issue counterfeit metallic coins that were accepted as precious metal. Of course, even in the most primitive legal system, issuing a false document for fraudulent purposes would be a criminal act, one that could only be undertaken with impunity by the king himself or by someone authorized by him to do so. In any event, it was through such collaboration between a greedy monarch and a dishonest banker that fractional-reserve banking became legalized; the king offered the banker immunity from fraud prosecution (and protection from anyone who objected) in exchange for the banker's financial backing.

Both assured the public that it was all right for the goldsmith to issue more receipts than he had gold on deposit, because he would retain sufficient gold in relation to the deposit receipts outstanding to redeem that portion of the total that (he expected) might be presented at any one time for redemption.

As long as the banker is moderate in his issues of counterfeit deposit receipts, the depreciating effect on the value of other receipts outstanding is little noticed by the public; nevertheless it does gradually occur. When he is immoderate and the effects become much noticed by the public, or when for whatever reason large numbers of depositors become wary of his solvency and demand their gold, then one of two things must happen. Either he becomes bankrupt and is able to pay out only the "fractional reserve" of the full amount owing, or, before that happens he anticipates the impending disaster and calls upon the king to issue a decree to close the bank, thereby preventing the depositors, at least temporarily, from submitting their demands.* As long as the bank remains closed, its receipts (banknotes) will continue to circulate only at a heavy and increasing discount compared to their face amount gold value and compared to other banknotes that are less suspect (for example, the U.S. dollar in comparison to gold and foreign currencies since August 1971).

Usually, during the closure, the banker himself, or in some cases the king, would arrange for a temporary loan of gold from some other area which would be acquired in quantity sufficient to meet all demands for redemption; the bank would then reopen and meet the onrush of the bank run. Then some depositors, seeing that the redemptions were being made,

*This was precisely the explanation for Franklin D. Roosevelt's order closing U.S. banks in 1933.

wouldn't bother to present their notes; while others who had presented their notes for redemption would shortly return the gold to the bank's depositories to take advantage of the greater convenience of the newly acceptable banknotes.

After a time, the banker and/or king, seeing that the notes were circulating satisfactorily at a relatively small discount from their face amount gold value, would become encouraged to further inflate the notes in circulation, and the cycle would repeat itself. Each successive cycle would tend to increase the discount percentage of the banknote versus physical gold, and would depreciate still more the exchange value of both the banknotes and gold as compared to the prior cycle.

The Misuse of Double-Entry Bookkeeping

Soon after the introduction of the fractional-reserve banking idea, bankers began to apply this same wrong principle in their bookkeeping. Previously, the goldsmiths loaned out their own gold to their customers for the payment of interest upon the loan. They also accepted long-term "time" deposits from some customers, paying them a relatively small rate of interest for the deposit, and used these funds to grant shorter-term loans at a relatively higher rate of interest to other customers. This procedure, along with legitimate banknote issue, was the original concept of banking and was an economically sound one which produced no inflationary effects upon the money supply nor any depreciating effects upon the value of money.

With the application of the fractional-reserve idea to the bank's bookkeeping procedures, however, banks began to loan money in the form of deposit credits to borrowers in a total amount greater than the total amount of actual deposits plus the banker's capital. Thus, with the collaboration of the local ruler, bankers acquired a further exemption from fraud prosecution, in exchange for providing such unsecured loans to the king himself more or less whenever the king demanded them.

The fact that the banker was fraudulently loaning money

that didn't exist by making balancing but fictitious loan and deposit entries in his books, was more obscure to the public than the issuance of a surplus of banknotes, and its effects were even less visible to the public. Nevertheless, every such entry had the same inflationary effect on the money supply that an equal issue of banknotes would have had, and every such entry had a depreciating effect on the value of all money units already in circulation.

In private hands, unaided by the ruler or state, credit is never inflationary. Why? Because it does not increase the money supply; it only moves the *use* of *existing real money value* from where it temporarily is not needed to where it temporarily is needed, and back again when the temporary need is fulfilled and money payment is made.*

Only in the hands of the state, with credit based on tax power, not on value owned, and in the hands of banks exempted by the state from fraud prosecution, with credit based on deceit, not on value owned, can credit be artificially and arbitrarily increased by the simple turning of a printing press or the mere posting of false debit and credit bookkeeping entries.

Further, based upon the counterfeit values created and upon fractional-reserve banking procedures, the process can be repeated again and again (with built-in interest-earning incentives to the banker to do so) and pyramided until the accelerating monetary inflation becomes runaway, leading to the destruction of the money values of all money substitutes.

The foregoing description of fractional-reserve banking, as to both banknotes and deposits, is an accurate functional description of money and banking as it existed in the 18th century and early in the 19th century. This discussion is not a concrete historical account, but a presentation of these developments in a logical sequence in order to convey an

*Credit itself is not money. Debt itself is not money. Credit is a money amount receivable, but not yet received, by one party; debt is a money amount payable, but not yet paid, by another party; each is, therefore, the opposite side of a *temporarily incomplete* transaction, one which, when completed by the transfer of *money* (the *final means of payment*), extinguishes both the credit and the debt.

understanding of money substitutes and fractional-reserve banking.

Now let's look at the actual method by which governments today inflate the money supply through the banking system.

Fractional-Reserve Banking Today

In former times, profligate states (especially those lacking a central bank) often simply printed additional currency notes to make up the deficit between their current tax revenues and their current spending programs. In today's bookkeeping economy, with modern well-developed financial markets (and a central bank), however, the creation of fiat money is done in a much subtler and simpler manner (from the standpoint of the state). It simply borrows the money it needs. The deficit between revenues and expenditures is "monetized."

In the United States, this means that the Federal Reserve Bank buys U.S. Treasury bonds for its own account and "pays" for them by simply crediting the Treasury's account — a bookkeeping technique well known to embezzlers.

When the Treasury writes a check on its account at one of the 12 Federal Reserve Banks and pays a supplier or welfare recipient, the "money" enters the commercial banking system. Let's trace it through the system; not one person in a thousand knows this technical process, and even fewer understand its significance.

The recipient can do basically one of two things with the government check: he can simply cash the check, take the cash and not spend it. In this case, since the money supply (narrowly defined, M1) is defined as currency in circulation outside banks plus demand deposits, it simply increases by the amount of the government check. Or, he can cash the check and spend the cash, or he can deposit the check in his deposit account. Suppose he does the latter. A new deposit is created in the commercial banking system and since demand deposits are part of M1, the money supply increases by the amount of the check. *But* in this case it doesn't stop there.

The deposit now becomes part of the bank's reserves and because of the fractional-reserve banking system, the bank only has to keep on hand a small fraction of the deposit — currently around 12 percent for deposit accounts. What the bank does then is lend out the equivalent of 88 percent of the demand deposit to, say, another customer of the bank whose deposit account is credited. Now we have the original deposit addition to the money supply plus the new credit in the second deposit account. When a check is written on one of these accounts and deposited in another bank, it then becomes another addition to the money supply and an addition to that bank's reserves and continues until, after the process repeats five or six times, the money supply is increased by a multiple of the original government check. Recently the multiplier has been around 2.5 the initial injection.

For example, assume the Federal Reserve Bank takes on $50 billion of new federal deficit in a given year. The increase in money supply (M1) should turn out to be around $125 billion (50 x 2.5). This explanation only elaborates the effect on M1, the narrowly defined money supply; M2, a broader definition including time deposits, through a similar process more highly leveraged (because of lower reserve requirements) has a multiplier of 6.

Under the Monetary Control Act of 1980 the Fed is empowered to reduce reserve requirements still further and, for the first time, is further empowered to purchase and monetize debt securities issued by private corporations, banks, municipalities, states, etc. In other words this act authorizes the Fed to buy any IOUs it chooses in unlimited amounts, and to create Federal-Reserve dollars and dollar credits in unlimited amounts to "pay" for them!

Paper Money
Backed by Paper

There is only one cause of inflation; it is officially — but not constitutionally — authorized counterfeiting of money, the official issue of paper money substitutes that are not fully backed

Genuine paper money is redeemable in the actual assets it represents, generally gold or silver. The 1922 gold certificate shown above states clearly: "This certifies that there have been deposited in the Treasury of the United States twenty dollars in gold coin, payable to the bearer on demand." The 1896 silver certificate carries the same promise. In effect, these certificates are warehouse receipts for the coins.

by and redeemable in the real lawful money they purport to represent.

Redeemable money substitutes backed by actual money (e.g., gold or silver) are the only form of genuine official paper money. Such paper money derives its ability to function as a money substitute from the fact that it is backed by real money assets and is a valid claim on them. This is the key characteristic of a genuine money. It is also the characteristic that distinguishes genuine paper money from counterfeit paper money.

Genuine paper money is fully redeemable. Official

counterfeit paper money, originally at least, carries the promise of redeemability *which the issuer knows to be fraudulent*. Official paper money which is not redeemable and which does not carry even the (false) promise of redeemability is worse than common counterfeit paper money — it is fiat money; fake, worthless paper which your government orders you to accept as though it were genuine.

Briefly defined, fiat money is simply fractional-reserve banking carried to its logical extreme. It is money-substitute paper with no money backing whatever. It is not even a promise to pay money; it is only a paper promise to pay paper (which is patent nonsense). Fiat money is what is left when the redeemable fractional-reserve money becomes so fractionalized that the central bank issuer defaults on its redemption promise because, for actual or anticipated lack of specie (gold or silver), it is no longer able or willing to make specie payments.

Through the long series of perverse modifications to the rules and practices of monetary institutions since 1913, the currencies of the Western nations, once fully backed by gold, were rendered first partially counterfeit and, since 1971, completely fraudulent fiat paper.

Such fiat money will continue to circulate for a time after the cessation of redeemability if two or more of the following conditions exist: (a) the public generally is unaware of the cessation of redeemability and/or unaware of its significance; (b) there is no immediate apparent and convenient alternative available; (c) the hope remains that it will again become redeemable; (d) the recipient expects that he can pass it on at a value near his acquisition value; and, lastly and least important, (e) the state decrees that it must be accepted in exchange.

At least *two* of the above five conditions are required in order for fiat money to continue circulating because the last one, the decree of the state, does not work alone. Each of the first four is obviously temporary, *viz*: (a) the public eventually does become aware; (b) alternatives do exist: gold and silver and perhaps other suitable "things of value" and, as time goes on, they become increasingly obvious and convenient; (c) hope, unfulfilled, diminishes; (d) the expectation of being able

to "pass it on" at near-acquisition value declines in proportion
to how rapidly the currency loses value. In the absence of
redeemability, and in the absence of the residuals-of-
redeemability (above items b, c and d) velocity increases as
people exercise the only convertibility left open to them: a
panic flight from currencies, converting their rapidly
depreciating paper money by purchasing real values (goods
and services) in the marketplace.

All national paper currencies today are 100-percent irredeemable fiat money and, as recognition of their fraudulent
natures and actual valuelessness sinks into the public
awareness, their exchange value in the marketplace will sink,
erratically to be sure, to, or very near to, zero.

There is no limit whatever on the amounts of fiat money
issued and/or credited to government checking accounts.
Thus, the state has unlimited *nominal* spending power which
inflates the money supply and depreciates the value of all
paper money on an accelerating basis.

Exporting U.S. domestic inflation

CHAPTER FOUR

The Roots of Global Runaway Inflation

The government consists of a gang of men exactly like you and me. They have, taking one with another, no special talent for the business of government, they have only a talent for getting and holding office. Their principal device to that end is to search out groups who pant and pine for something they can't get and promise to give it to them. Nine times out of ten, that promise is worth nothing. The tenth time it is made good by looting A to satisfy B. In other words, government is a broker in pillage, and every election is a sort of an advance auction of the sale of stolen goods.

—H.L. Mencken

Since 1965 U.S. federal spending has increased more than sixfold. The largest portion of the increase has been caused by skyrocketing welfare transfer payments.

Federal welfare spending increased steadily in the 1960s, tripling over the decade. In the 1970s it exploded. In 1970 it was $60 billion. By 1973 it reached $95 billion, and by 1976 it had jumped to $158 billion. In 1979, welfare expenditures exceeded $200 billion, becoming the largest single item in the federal budget and devouring over 40 percent of total federal spending.

Welfare transfer payments are doubly damaging: they penalize enterprise and production and reward idleness and consumption. Thus, even when fully covered by direct taxes, they push prices up by decreasing the supply of goods and services while increasing demand. When financed by deficit spending or inflationary fiat dollars, they are triply damaging because they add still more nominal demand on the decreased supply, boosting prices even more.

43

Runaway U.S. Deficit Spending

Federal budget surpluses would appear to have had their day. Excepting 1969, we had deficits in all other years of the 1960s. There were deficits *every* year in the 1970s and the total for the past ten years was an incredible $373 billion! As a result, federal debt outstanding has *doubled* in the same period and interest on this debt has become the third largest item in the federal budget (after welfare and defense).

Chart 2
Federal Spending, 1970-81

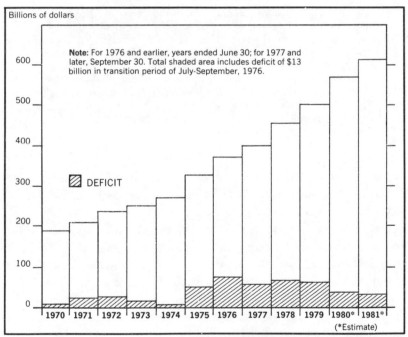

Billions of dollars

Note: For 1976 and earlier, years ended June 30; for 1977 and later, September 30. Total shaded area includes deficit of $13 billion in transition period of July-September, 1976.

DEFICIT

(*Estimate)

Source: U.S. Office of Management and Budget

Further, the deficit figures shown in Chart 2 are only the tip-of-the-iceberg "official deficits." They do not include "off-budget" borrowing and spending which, since the early 1970s has moved from a few billion dollars annually into high double-digit billions.

And, there is still more. The official deficits also do not include unfunded federal liabilities for military and civil service pensions, insurance commitments and other obligations, accruing to the tune of hundreds of billions of dollars annually. Sooner or later, all of these officially uncounted deficit dollars must stand up and be counted.

The real federal debt on which interest is paid (excluding future liabilities) is easily in excess of $1,000 billion. Interest payments alone now exceed the amount of the total federal budget as recently as 1960. And continued deficit spending doubly aggravates the problem, first by increasing the total amount of debt upon which interest must be paid, and secondly, by pushing interest rates higher for everyone — including the federal super state.

In the four years 1972-76, interest on the federal debt doubled from $20.6 billion to $41.3 billion; in only three years, through 1979, it had nearly doubled again to about $80 billion. Today it takes nearly 20 percent of the total federal budget. With much of the debt issues rolled-over in 1979 and early 1980 at record-high interest rates, and with record Treasury borrowing this year and next, with the outlook for interest rates to soar to new record high levels in 1981, and with Treasury debt issues being mostly short-term, we can expect that the next doubling, to $160 billion or more, will come within two years (1982); then the next doubling in about one more year. Then. . . ?

Runaway Federal Debt

As described earlier, the monetization of federal deficits is accomplished through the agency of the Federal Reserve System. In order to "pay" for the debt securities it purchases, either from the Treasury directly or, most often, from commercial banks, the Fed simply creates (counterfeits) a corresponding "deposit amount" on its books in the form of a credit to the seller. When the seller — the U.S. Treasury — writes a check on its account at the Fed, the proceeds end up in the commercial banking system as reserves and thus increase the banking system's ability to expand loans, deposits, and therefore the overall money supply, by a multiple.

The Fed is entirely the handmaiden of the U.S. Treasury. It

must buy U.S. Treasury issues from the Treasury and/or the banking system (and counterfeit the credits to do so) whenever and in any amounts necessary to accommodate new Treasury issues and to support the nominal market value of already outstanding issues.

To the extent that the Federal Treasury's bonds and notes are purchased by the public (as most of them were until recently), the total impact is not immediately inflationary. What happens then is that purchasing power is simply temporarily transferred from the purchasers of those bonds and notes to the state.

To the extent that these Treasury bonds and notes are purchased by the banking system, however, the inflationary impact is even greater than the direct printing of fiat currency would be because the bonds and notes, in part financed by "created" Federal Reserve credit, go into the banking system's fractional reserves and become the basis for issuance of money and credit in a multiple amount—providing commercial banks still more credit dollars to buy still more Treasury debt issues, etc.

In actual practice, most of the public's dealings in Treasury bonds and notes are rollovers, that is, purchases of new bonds and notes are made with the proceeds of maturing bonds and notes. Nevertheless, each new issue is larger than the issues being retired and, on balance, since 1971, the non-bank public's holdings of federal debt issues increased 60 percent to over $350 billion, while foreign holdings doubled to $100 billion, and commercial banks' holdings were up 33 percent to over $150 billion (see Chart 3). These accumulations have soaked up much of the federal deficit financing that otherwise would have to be purchased and monetized by the Federal Reserve Bank. In the same period the Fed's monetized holdings of Treasury debt issues increased only 26 percent to $138 billion.

At some point, a major part of the over $500 billion of debt instruments held privately could flood into the Fed and boost monetary inflation by hundreds of billions in a single year. Public and commercial banks' holdings continued to increase until mid-1977. Since then, however, private credit demand has increased enormously, and banks have been unloading

Chart 3
Ownership of U.S. Government Securities

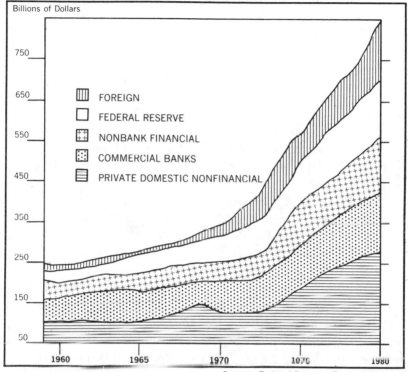

Source: Federal Reserve Bank of St. Louis

their Treasury bonds on the Fed. Why hasn't this yet had an effect on the money supply? Simply because the foreign component shown in Chart 3 has played an increasingly stronger role in moderating U.S. domestic inflation throughout the 1970s.

Exporting U.S. Domestic Inflation

We have escaped extreme runaway inflation thus far chiefly because of the dollar's singular position in international money markets. The U.S. has been able to engage in massive deficit spending right through the seventies without incurring severe domestic inflation, simply by exporting its inflation overseas.

Although the dollar ceased to be officially redeemable in gold in 1971, foreign central banks continued to behave as if it were. They upheld the Bretton Woods system of fixed exchange rates, whereby every currency was valued in terms of the dollar.

Having built up huge dollar reserves prior to 1971 the foreign central banks were compelled to support the dollar just to maintain the value of these reserves. When the number of dollars coming on to the market threatened to drive the value of their own currencies up (and the value of their U.S. dollars reserves down), they intervened, buying dollars with their own currencies.

However, in 1973 the flood of dollars reached such proportions (for that time) that central banks finally withdrew their support. The dollar was devalued, and the system of fixed exchange rates came to an end.

Under the floating exchange rate system that ensued, each country was supposed to let the markets determine its currency's exchange rate. In practice, however, the unceasing flow of dollars again threatened to drive the exchange rates of all major foreign currencies up. Again, central banks were forced to intervene, printing increasing quantities of their own currencies with which to purchase dollars, in a vain attempt to shore up the dollar's value. In this manner, U.S. domestic money inflation was exported to every major foreign nation.

Chart 4 tells a powerful story about the source and magnitude of today's worldwide runaway inflation. Total international "reserves" have more than quintupled since March 1968, when the international redeemability of the dollar was effectively abandoned. Significantly, the foreign exchange component (almost exclusively dollars) has increased by a multiple of almost 10. In other words, virtually *all* of the increase is in (newly created) fiat paper dollars!

The predictable effect of over three decades of virtually non-stop deficit spending has been an inevitable — and practically uninterrupted — decline in the value of the dollar, i.e., a rise in prices. In the last 40 years, prices have dropped only twice (1949 and 1955) and then by less than one percent.

Chart 4
International Monetary Reserves

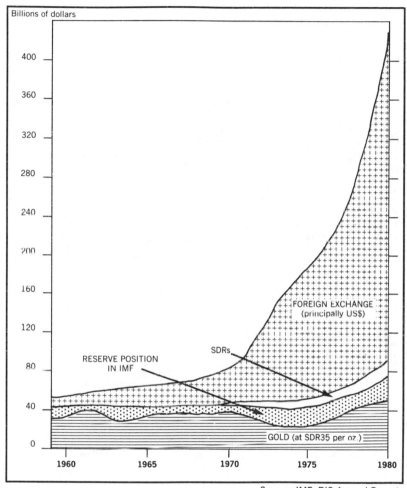

Source: IMF; BIS Annual Reports

Every other year the general price level has risen, by nearly 10 percent per year in recent years. The effect on the dollar's purchasing power has been dramatic (Chart 5). Today's dollar is worth about 20 percent of its 1939 value — and only half the value of the dollar just 10 years ago.

The depreciating value of the dollar is felt by everyone — including the state. The inflationists' answer is to inflate at successively higher levels in order to finance successively

Chart 5
Depreciation of the U.S. Dollar

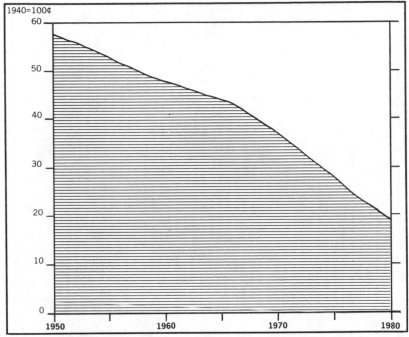

Source: Consumer Price Index

higher levels of federal spending. In the early stages of runaway inflation, the state gains spending power in both nominal and real terms because the rate of monetary inflation is greater than the rate of monetary depreciation. After a time, however, the public reacts by increasing the velocity of money and the rate of monetary depreciation (price inflation) catches up to and then exceeds the rate of monetary inflation. This is the watershed point. This is the point after which it becomes impossible for the state to gain spending power in real terms, no matter how rapidly it accelerates the rate of monetary inflation.

Global Monetary Blackmail

Entirely because of habit and foreign official inertia since 1971, the dollar has continued to be (1) the international monetary reserve currency, (2) the foreign exchange intervention currency, and (3) the leading exchange currency in international trade.

The effect of central banks' intervention in exchange markets has in each case been the opposite of that intended: generally, the weak currencies have become weaker and the strong have become stronger since 1971.

The British pound (-21 percent) is a prime example of the former, and the Swiss franc (+131 percent) and German mark (+82 percent) of the latter.

The decline in the pound and the lira strengthened international demand for the dollar still further. More importantly, it led to the eventual abandonment of the pound by the OPEC countries in favor of the dollar. And the massively higher OPEC oil price has required correspondingly larger dollar-denominated payments by all the oil-deficit countries.

> The key. . .is the huge increase in oil prices — beyond what it is doing to the world economy *per se*. . .since oil contracts are traditionally denominated in U.S. dollars, the enormous increase in the price of oil has further increased the pivotal role of the dollar all over the world. Far from waning after the Bretton Woods system died, the dollar — thanks to oil — is even more the "numeraire" reserve currency than ever before.*

Continued and growing international demand for dollars has relatively reduced the domestic money supply, moderating U.S. price inflation. Also, and of equal importance, the OPEC countries and Western European and Japanese central banks have placed the bulk of their dollar holdings into U.S. Treasury securities rather than into commercial bank deposits and/or other U.S. investments that would boost the domestic money supply. Were it not for this, the Federal Reserve System would be sopping up Treasury notes in even greater amounts, and boosting the U.S. money supply even more than it has done.

Thus, since 1971, the U.S. has experienced the best of both monetary worlds: it has continued to enjoy all the international advantages of having a redeemable currency and at the same time has not been restrained either by the burden of

Business Week, October 3, 1977, p. 7.

redemption or by any effective restraining measures by foreign official dollar holders. Conversely, the other Western trading nations and Japan until recently have suffered the worst of both monetary worlds: they have pretended that the irredeemable paper dollars they hold as reserves are still a store of value while watching them fall in value; they have continued to pay out their own currencies to buy more paper dollars; and in the process they have been paying out *real goods and services* for huge and increasing amounts of this depreciating fiat paper. How long will they continue to cooperate in their own impoverishment?

To understand their continued participation in the global fiat fiasco, one has only to consider the alternative faced by the Western nations and Japan: *chaos*. Without a functioning international medium of exchange (e.g., the U.S. dollar), every nation in the world would be faced with economic (and consequential political) chaos. In theory, the other major industrial nations could go it alone, apart from the U.S., by forming a new international or regional (e.g., European) monetary unit and system. However, political jealousy and rivalry have so far precluded agreement — much less implementation. Still less is the likelihood of any durability for such a system in the absence of full and complete U.S. participation and cooperation.

Unfortunately, I believe, the crisis-postponement that has been achieved has set the stage for higher levels of money inflation and ultimately a crisis of greater magnitude in the future.

The official counterfeiting of money

CHAPTER FIVE

Why Inflation Will Not Be Stopped

No subject is so much discussed today — or so little understood — as inflation. The politicians in Washington talk of it as if it were some horrible visitation from without, over which they had no control — like a flood, a foreign invasion, or a plague. It is something they are always promising to "fight" — if Congress or the people will only give them the "weapons" or "a strong law" to do the job.

Yet the plain truth is that our political leaders have brought on inflation by their own money and fiscal policies. They are promising to fight with their right hand the conditions brought on with their left.

—Henry Hazlitt
What You Should Know About Inflation

One of the reasons I have been saying emphatically for several years that inflation is running away, and will continue to do so, is that virtually all of the "economic advisors" to officials are inflationists. That is, they believe that some degree of inflation is both necessary and desirable for the economy.

In Chapter 3 I defined inflation as "any increase of the money supply." Any embellishment of this definition is completely unnecessary and only tends to confuse the subject matter. The most common embellishment (one that has been included in virtually every economics textbook published since the late 1920s) is to add the qualification ". . .which is in excess of the rate of productivity increase." This inflationist "textbook" definition of inflation implies that (a) the state has a prior claim on the fruits of productivity increases (created by technological advances), and (b) the state can be trusted to limit its inflation of the money supply to only that small productivity-increase percentage (normally 3 to 4 percent per

55

year). The first implication is, to say the least, open to question and recent inflation rates have clearly disproved the second.

In the absence of monetary inflation the benefits of increased productivity flow firstly and directly to those initially responsible for the increased productivity; secondly and indirectly to the consuming public in the form of lower competitive prices for the products of those particular producers; and ultimately to the whole consuming population in the form of generally lower prices. That is, the value of the money units and of the whole money supply gradually increases. Thus, through market action, an unchanged supply of (more valuable) money accommodates increasing levels of production and trade. (Hence also does the market reward the thrifty with a higher future value of their savings.)

In the presence of monetary inflation the benefits of increased productivity are siphoned away by those responsible for artificially inflating the money supply and, because the inflation rate exceeds the productivity increase rate, the consuming public is disadvantaged by generally higher prices and robbed through the surreptitious theft of real money-value from their nominally unchanged savings.

Inflationist Arguments (against a stable money supply)

Nevertheless, the inflationists continue to argue that it is necessary to have regular increases in the supply of money in order to facilitate the successively higher levels of production. This argument is both capricious and specious. It is capricious because it is an insincere attempt to demonstrate a need for inflation of the money supply in order to justify the inflationary fiscal and monetary policies of the state. It is specious because it focuses attention on only one of three variables involved in monetary exchange and ignores the other two. It emphasizes the quantity of money and ignores both the value of money and the velocity (turnover) of money. The truth is that increased levels of trade can be monetarily accommodated in any one of three ways: (a) an increased quantity of money with an unchanged price level and unchanged velocity, (b) an increased value of money (lower price level) with an unchanged quantity of money and unchanged velocity, or (c) an increased velocity of money with unchanged value and quantity.

The inflationists' preoccupation with the quantity of money stems from the same root as all other political fallacies: the attempt to get something for nothing. The inflationists' interest is in "spending" the newly printed currency — an obvious immediate benefit to those in control of the presses, one that they play down. A portion of the spending power is used to distribute largess to the voting population — an obvious immediate benefit to these recipients, one that the inflationists play up.

In social science, as in physical science, for every action there is a reaction. For every benefit there is a cost. The distinction is that in social science they are seldom equal. Generally, social action which is voluntary (as to all of those affected) produces benefits greater than the costs (temporary exception: a failing business). Invariably, social action which is coerced (including deception) produces benefits lesser than the costs (no exceptions).

All of the inflationist-statist arguments are aimed at inverting these realities.

Inflation, at all stages, creates distortions, resource misallocations and disorder generally. In its later stages it causes labor strikes, commercial turmoil, international trade wars, urban strife, food riots and, sometimes, shooting wars. On a global basis, we are approaching those later stages.

Runaway Inflation — and Depression

Once the inflationists' arguments become generally accepted and operative, it is only a matter of time until inflation accelerates and becomes runaway inflation. Runaway inflation *begins* when the state's monetary inflation rate exceeds the society's overall rate of productivity increase, thereby depreciating all money values and requiring the state to inflate at successively higher rates in order to finance successively higher levels of spending.

Briefly defined, an *advanced* runaway inflation is a monetary inflation which has accelerated to the point that the rate of monetary depreciation races ahead of the rate of monetary inflation. This happened in 1973, and again in 1979; each time it was followed by a recession or depression.

Chart 6
Inflation in Money and Prices

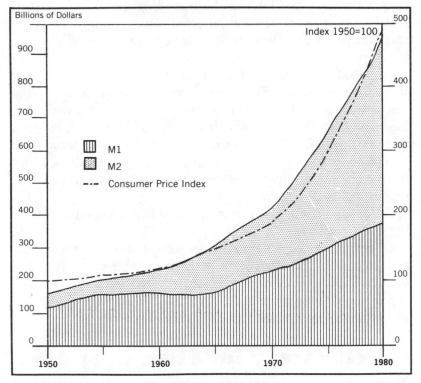

In real terms, an inflationary depression is indistinguishable from a deflationary depression. In both cases production and incomes decline in real terms ; in both cases liquidity problems proliferate; in both cases widespread bankruptcies occur. The distinction between a deflationary and an inflationary depression is this: in a deflationary depression, production, incomes and living standards generally decline both in real terms and in nominal money terms; in an inflationary depression, production, incomes and living standards generally also decline in real terms while at the same time all of these show increases in nominal money terms.

Inflation depreciates the purchasing value of the official currency and simultaneously appreciates the value of the officially abandoned real money (gold and silver in our millennium). Over time the rate of fiat money issue tends to increase, as government spending in excess of tax receipts increases, causing a coincident but greater rate of depreciation in the market value of each unit and of the nominally increasing total stock of paper currency. This, in turn, forces the officials to increase the rate of counterfeiting again and again in order to try to cover the soaring cost of underfunded but already budgeted programs. The process then feeds on itself and ultimately destroys the currency completely, the currency ceases to be money by anybody's definition, and this pushes the paper money price of gold and silver into the stratosphere.

In the earlier stages of runaway inflation, the inflationists' answer is to impose wage and price controls. As economist George Reisman has observed, this "is as illogical as would be an attempt to deal with expanding pressure in a boiler by means of manipulating the needle in the boiler's pressure gauge."*

Controls Don't Work

Both economic theory and historical experience tell us that wage and price controls do not work, that all attempts to make them work have resulted not only in failure but in serious damage as well. Yet, Mr. Nixon's early 1970s controls program was superficially credited with success and many other Western nations have since emulated these policies. How, and why, has this come about?

*From the Introduction to his book *The Government Against the Economy* (1980: Caroline House Publishers, Ottawa, Ill.).

Several independent economic studies in the U.S. have demonstrated that wage and price trends *existing at the time the Nixon controls were imposed* would have led to about the same wage and price experience in the U.S. in 1972 without the controls program. Thus, the "success" of a moderation in the U.S. rate of wage and price advances in 1972 was a result of market forces already in motion, for which Mr. Nixon's bureaucrats took unearned credit. Further, when the controls were abandoned, every businessman was thereby encouraged to raise his prices as much as his market would bear, immediately rather than later, out of a fear that controls might again be suddenly imposed. Many did just that and the overall effect contributed to double-digit price escalations in 1973-74.

Today, with the Nixon controls still fresh in memory, and fearing Carter's greater apparent predisposition toward controls, businessmen in various industries are raising prices in anticipation of new price controls.

The Imposition of Credit Controls

Under the Credit Control Act of 1969 (Public Law 91-151), the President has the power to direct the Federal Reserve Board (FRB) to control all credit allocation in the U.S. Unlike wage and price controls, which would require new Congressional authority, President Carter was able to implement these powers with a simple executive order.

Specifically, Section 205(a) gives the President these broad authorities: "Whenever the President determines that such action is necessary or appropriate for the purpose of preventing or controlling inflation generated by the extension of credit in an excessive volume, the President may authorize the Board to regulate and control *any or all extensions of credit*." (Emphasis added.)

Section 205(b) further states: "The Board may, in administering this Act, utilize the services of the Federal Reserve Banks and any other agencies, federal or state, which are available and appropriate."

Section 206 itemizes some of the controls:

(1) require transactions or persons or classes of either to be registered or licensed.

(2) prescribe appropriate limitations, terms and conditions for any such registration or license.

(3) provide the suspension of any such registration or license for violation of any provision thereof or of any regulation, rule or order prescribed under this Act.

(4) prescribe appropriate requirements as to the keeping of records and as to the form, contents or substantive provisions of contracts, liens or any relevant documents.

(5) prohibit solicitations by creditors which would encourage evasion or avoidance of the requirements of any regulation, license or registration under this Act.

(6) prescribe the maximum amount of credit which may be extended on, or in connection with, any loan, purchase or other extension of credit.

(7) prescribe the maximum rate of interest, maximum maturity, minimum periodic payment, maximum period between payments and any other specification or limitation of the terms and conditions of any extension of credit.

(8) prescribe the methods of determining purchase prices or market values or other bases for computing permissible extensions of credit or required down payment.

(9) prescribe special or different terms, conditions or exemptions with respect to new or used goods, minimum original cash payments, temporary credits which are merely incidental to cash purchases, payment or deposits usable to liquidate credits, and other adjustments or special situations.

The excerpts from this Act should be more than enough to convince you that imposition of even a small portion of these powers will have a profoundly negative impact on commodity markets in the U.S. and the economy as a whole.

Overall, the financial community views the imposition of the Credit Control Act as deflationary, especially as it is accompanied by claims that monetary policy is going to continue on a restrictive course.

The government's timing in imposing credit controls in 1980 was as bad as its imposition of the wage and price freeze was in 1971; now, as before, the economy is already beginning a decided downtrend, and the result will be to worsen the present recession, which promises to become a depression of far greater magnitude than any other since the 1930s.

Why Controls Make Things Worse

Price controls do not work; and here is why. The economic profile for each and every product or service, including credit, is described by three variable elements: (1) Prices, (2) Supply, (3) Demand. In a free market all three fluctuate, with interrelated effect, as follows:

Change: *Results:*
If P trend is ⟶ then S tends ⟶ and D tends ⟶
If P trend is ↘ then S tends ↘ and D tends ↗
If S trend is ↗ then P tends ↘ and D tends ↗
If S trend is ⟶ then P tends ↗ and D tends ⟶
If D trend is ↗ then P tends ↗ and S tends ↗
If D trend is ⟶ then P tends ⟶ and S tends ⟶

In the real economic world, each element (P, S and D), for each and every product or service in each and every market, has a direction and momentum of its own, at any given time. The motion of each element is moderated, exaggerated or overcome by the combined effect of the motion of the other two elements. This is a complicated process even for one single product or service, and enormously more complicated for a whole economy. Fortunately, in a free market, the process is automatic. When a price control is imposed, one of three kinds of results occurs: (1) If the market forces call for the price of a particular item to remain about even, then the control has no important effect. (2) If market forces call for a lower price (and this is prevented) then a surplus of that item will appear. (3) If market forces call for the price to rise (and this is prevented), then the P momentum is shifted to cause an artificial relative decrease in supply and/or an artificial relative increase in demand, causing first a shortage and then a black market, at a price higher than the free market price would have been.

If price controls are in operation at a time when, overall,

they have no effect, or very little effect (as in the U.S. in 1972), and they are continued long enough, then it is only a question of time before the underlying market forces change and surpluses or shortages and black market prices result.

Effective price restrictions are impossible without complete control also over supply and demand. The official response to controls-caused shortages and black markets may be to end the controls, as Nixon did, or to extend them to encompass control of supplies (forced production quotas) and/or of consumption rates (allocations and rationing). If re-elected, the "puppeteer" Carter administration will probably push controls to that extreme, judging by the precedent of the pattern of fascistic, push-pull manipulations in his "energy program."

Meanwhile the underlying problem, inflationary expansion of the money supply through monetization of federal deficits, continues unchecked — providing the fuel for renewed surges of wage and price inflation in the future. The real dangers of price and wage control programs increase in proportion to the time they are in effect. The chief dangers are that they obscure the need for a solution to the real problem — deficit-spending-based monetary inflation — and that they cause malutilization of capital and labor resources, misdirecting production, and, in company with continued monetary inflation, lead ultimately to a hyperinflationary depression.

These damaging long-run consequences of inflation, and of price and wage controls, are widely rather well understood by many economists (including some of those advising politicians); yet, because, in the context of runaway welfare spending domestically and a paper-only international monetary non-system, each national political leader is without any unilateral solution for his domestic inflation problem, and because collectively these officials cannot agree to adopt a non-inflationary international monetary system, the world is headed deeper into the quagmire of various forms of domestic price and wage controls and international trade restrictions. These trends, if continued, will lead directly into a worldwide hyperinflationary depression and, perhaps indirectly, to Nuclear War. The big unknown is how far we have already travelled toward the edge of this precipice?

The Way to Stop Inflation and Depression

While my many warnings that inflation is running away and will continue to do so have been timely and correct, it is nevertheless important to understand that, but for the political reasons cited, inflation could be stopped. Further, it could be stopped quickly and with less damage earlier than later.

The "Austrian School" economists, particularly Ludwig von Mises,* have demonstrated this very clearly and precisely. Any inflation, at any stage, can be stopped in its tracks by (1) an official and immediate slashing of central government spending down to the level of current tax receipts (i.e., a balanced budget); and (2) an official and unequivocal stop-the-presses freeze on the money factory (the Federal Reserve System).

The inflationists argue falsely that these steps would cause massive unemployment and plunge the nation into a (worse) depression. This is an unproven assertion that, no matter how often repeated, is simply not so. What these steps would do is put an end to the distortions that monetary inflation causes, and permit large numbers of people who are now mis-employed in non-productive and/or uneconomic activity to change their employment into economic, productive endeavors; further these two steps would permit the realloca-tion of capital, fuel and other resources that are presently lock-ed into uneconomic uses into economic ones. The temporary unemployment and rash of bankruptcies that would take place are a consequence of the inflationary distortions of the past — which increase in number and magnitude the longer the infla-tion continues.

Finally these steps, contrary to the inflationists' arguments, would increase total spending and therefore total economic ac-tivity in real, meaningful terms; their effect on spending would be to permit a larger portion of total spending to be in private, prudent and productive hands and a lesser portion of the total in official, unproductive and wasteful hands.

*See his great work *Human Action* (3rd revised ed., 1966, Henry Regnery and Co., Chicago, Illinois).

Who (or What) is to Blame for Today's Inflation?

Does it matter? Yes, it does matter; if we don't know the who and the what underlying a problem, our understanding of the problem itself is a mere academic exercise — one that, instead of allowing us to make a proper beginning, leads only to fruitless efforts to repair the superstructure when the beginning of the problem and, therefore, the potential solution, lies in the foundation.

To begin with, the underlying error is the mistaken belief people have in the omnipotence of the state. This is the basic error that underlies virtually every large-scale social problem in the world today, including, but not only, the money problem. Specifically relating to the money problem, the basic error is the prevalent belief in a wholly wrong concept of money. As we have seen, money is not a legislative invention. It pre-dates all legislatures, it pre-dates all rulers. It is not something to be managed, rather it is something to be left alone. Once it is interfered with significantly by rulers and legislatures, the solution lies in the direction of their abdication, not in their further meddling.

The three corrupt elements of the American nation-state that are the motive force for today's runaway inflation are:

(1) Congressmen who get elected and re-elected by promising *more* spending favors to their constituents;

(2) Constituents, now a firmly entrenched clear voting majority, who vote for candidates promising them *more* federal largess; and

(3) Bureaucrats — the real rulers of the apparatus — who encourage both the Congressmen and the voters to spend *more* and who steadfastly *resist* — and even sabotage — any efforts to reduce their domains.

No one disputes the contention that the Federal Government has become an over-sized, cumbersome, fantastically inefficient monster. But this monster is not a creation of its own whims. It is, paradoxically, the creature of the selfsame — and normally righteous — ones who so piously declaim it must be whittled down.

Somebody remarked at the very start of this country's unique political system that government under a democratic order
can only grow in size — it can never shrink.

History has borne this out.

Every agency, bureau, commission, board, or department
has its built-in vested interests and its own potent constituency. This constituency runs from special committees on
Capitol Hill to the governmental body itself to that part of the
public which is presumed to be benefitted.

And every department, bureau, or agency in the executive
branch has its counterpart committee or sub-committee on
Capitol Hill. The survival of one depends upon the survival of
the other. Those who would voluntarily surrender their
authority in Washington are notable only for their scarcity.*

In view of the growing and now widespread recognition
that there is a money problem, one would expect that there
would be a growing official interest in seeking a genuine solution. Unfortunately, that is not the case. The reason it is not
the case is two-fold. On the one hand, the great majority of the
rulers, politicians, bankers and bureaucrats, thoroughly enjoy
exercising the arbitrary power that the existing (crumbling)
structure has put into their hands. Collectively, they would
rather preside over the destruction than abdicate. On the
other hand, the great majority of the public, while they have
no notion whatever of the nature of the problem or of the
benefits to them that would accrue from a solution, do still,
unfortunately, put too much faith in the "authorities." They
also enjoy the very visible benefits of the vast state deficit
spending programs.

Who (if Anyone) Can Stop Inflation?

Presidents obviously can't stop it; both Nixon and Ford
tried. Carter said he would by 1981 but you *cannot* count on
it. It is at best difficult to believe that Carter was even sincere
in his campaign promise to streamline the federal nation-state

*John Gerrity in *The Money Manager*, January 10, 1977.

and cut wasteful spending. Even if he was sincere, he has failed — as Lincoln, Wilson, Hoover, Roosevelt, Truman and Eisenhower, and others promised and failed in the past, and there is no reason to think that any new president would do any better. The motive force for the growth of the federal spending machine, and of federal spending, has long been beyond the control of any president.

The Federal Reserve can't stop it. The Fed has little actual leeway in what it does and can only act for a very short time to counter underlying fiscal and financial trends.

Bankers, with rare exceptions, want the inflationary money in ever-increasing amounts to replenish and expand their deposits and loan-investment portfolios.

Congressmen individually, hence collectively, want to spend, while repeal of any existing authorized spending is rarely even considered. To the extent that there is any interest in the problem at all generally, it is almost always directed not at eliminating inflation but at "controlling inflation." This is a wholly hopeless endeavor. Given the conditions that exist and the beliefs and motives of the actors, there is no way that the fiat money toboggan ride can be controlled or terminated short of the bottom of the pit.*

Some economic analysts think we can settle into an indexed low double-digit inflation that could go on for many years, such as has occurred in Brazil. This also is false for reasons explained by James Sibbet,** as follows:

> The reason they [Brazil] can do it is because they do not have the massive debt structure that we have. There is nothing to go

---

*International banker Nicholas Deak recently succinctly stated the reasons: "There is no such thing as a controlled inflation. In a democratic state, with controls, we cannot check inflation. . .it is the free forces of offer and demand which establish the purchasing power of the dollar (or in other countries their respective monies). We live in an uncontrolled inflationary world. Is it a runaway inflation? Every inflation in a large country with a democratic government is a runaway inflation. At the beginning it moves slowly but with time it gathers speed, faster and faster, and finally collapses. This is happening to our dollar."

**James Sibbet is a broker and editor of *Let's Talk Silver and Gold*. (1 year subscription: $46, to Sibbet Publications, 380 East Green Street, Financial Building, Suite 200, Pasadena, California 91101).

bankrupt in Brazil. There is a small but growing middle class, a tiny wealthy upper class, and the bulk of the people are poor by their own standards. These wage-earners are not bothered by inflation very much because their wages are indexed to the Consumer Price Index. The middle class also uses indexation to protect their contracts. The wealthy have long since bought up all the land and hedge against inflation by building and expanding plant facilities. The people that are hurt by inflation are the money lenders in Brazil. Those that do exist index their loans so they will not suffer. Also there are few people living on a fixed pension.

How different it is here in the U.S.A. where millions of people are dependent on a fixed pension. Millions more are money lenders. There is more wealth tied up in bonds and mortages than in any other form here. Another large segment of our wealth consists of savings and checking accounts. These too are a form of money lending. Never forget that the chief purpose of inflation is to tax money lenders. It just doesn't work that way in Brazil where there are so few money lenders.

Finally, to complete the list, can market action stop inflation via a spontaneous, massive liquidity crisis, forcing a deflation?

No, not in nominal terms; but it can and will cause depression in real terms — this is what happens in fits and starts in the middle stages (1974-75) (1980-?) and in massive terms in the final stages of a runaway inflationary depression (1985?) culminating in the complete destruction of currency-unit values.

The 1922-28 inflation and the 1929-32 deflation occurred in a different way and under entirely different circumstances from those of the recent past and now. Most importantly, in the 1920s the federal government and its spending (fully covered by tax revenues) were minuscule compared to now. Further, the 1920s monetary inflation stayed within the financial institutions, mostly in brokers' loans, and fueled a speculative boom in equity shares, *not* in prices generally — a boom that was fostered, then crushed, by an inexperienced and unbelievably inept Federal Reserve Board acting within a fiscal and monetary context that gave it wide latitude.

By contrast, in today's runaway inflation, the federal

government (and others) and its spending (not nearly covered by tax revenues) are gargantuan compared to then (or by any other comparison). Further, today's massive monetary inflation has spread, in a much longer time period, into virtually every element of financial and economic activity and has fueled an accelerating climb in the general price level which has been fostered by the pea-brained parasite ideology and massive dysfunctional mechanism of rampant statism — a statism to which the Federal Reserve Board is a helpless handmaiden, with virtually no latitude of action and absolutely no ability to resist the momentum of the underlying forces or to alter the course of the onrushing runaway inflation.

The redistribution of wealth

CHAPTER SIX

The Consequences of Inflation

Unfortunately, higher prices are *not* the most important consequence of the political creation of new monetary units. These
monetary units are endowed with full legal tender power. This
means that, by law, they have the same purchasing power as all
previously issued monetary units of the same name. New monetary units cannot be created by governments or anyone else without someone getting them and spending them first. Those who
first receive these newly created monetary units are able to go
out on the market and buy things they could not otherwise buy.
They can and do buy things which other people would have
bought with the money they had earned or saved. Thus every
political creation of new money transfers wealth from workers
and savers to those who are spending in the market place newly
created monetary units which no one has earned.
—Percy L. Greaves, Jr.
"Introduction," *Von Mises
On the Manipulation of Money and Credit*

The depreciation (and eventual destruction) of a currency's
value is not by any means the only bad effect of inflation. Even
in small annual percentage rates, monetary inflation over any
substantial period causes myriad mischiefs and sufferings to
innocent parties. Over the course of a generation or more some
of these little-recognized effects can be more damaging than
the more obvious price-level effect. Of course, the longer inflationary fiscal and monetary policies are continued, the more
the annual percentage rates rise and the more damaging inflation is in all of its harmful aspects. One of the most destructive
is the so-called business cycle — which, in fact, is a state
money and credit intervention cycle.

The outmoded historical economists (e.g., the Keynesians,
and Friedmanites) cannot cope with the monetary and
business-cycle aspects of either the national or international
economic situation today. Their theoretic concepts only deal

71

incompletely with situations for which there are clear historical precedents. Such limited concepts are wholly inadequate in the face of the numerous unprecedented conditions existing today.

The "Business Cycle"

It is a popular(ized) misconception that inflationary booms and deflationary busts are inherent in the free-market economy, and (since the New Deal and John Maynard Keynes) that the federal state can and should "manage the economy" through its fiscal and monetary policies to eliminate, or at least moderate, these twin evils of the "business cycle."

The key to unravelling this lies in a correct and complete definition of "free-market economy." Half-free is not free. And, the nearest the world has ever come to a free-market economy (e.g., the United States or Britain in the fourth quarter of the last century) was little more than half-free. Even then, the state taxed business, subsidized business, regulated business, operated business, dispensed favors, maintained standing armies, licensed fraudulent banking practices, licensed professions, educated children, supported charities, etc. Most people, including most economists, think that this was free-enterprise capitalism — a free-market economy. It wasn't.

Actually, the periodic booms and busts of history are *not* business cycles at all; they are *not* inherent in the free-market economy. They are associated with *fiat money* and credit cycles. The classical economists, particularly David Ricardo, recognized the essential nature of the cycles.

The Classical Explanation

In a nation having a fractional-reserve money and banking system, the cycle begins with a money and credit expansion. As the paper-money supply increases, money incomes and spending rise in nominal terms. Prices are bid up. There is an inflationary boom. Businesses appear to prosper, even the ill-conceived and poorly managed ones. Comparatively, as domestic prices rise, goods from abroad look cheap. Imports increase. Domestic products look expensive to foreigners. Exports decrease. Thus, there is a balance-of-trade deficit and a balance-of-payments deficit. Real money (gold or silver) is shipped abroad to make up the difference. Thus, the backing for the larger paper-money and credit supply becomes smaller. At some point the bankers of the nation become concerned that they may not be able to meet future demands for specie (gold and/or silver) payments — or, worse yet, that their depositors, entertaining the same fear, may make a run on the bank.

The bankers panic (inwardly at least); they stop making new loans, they stop re-issuing their own banknotes that come in. In short, they contract, they reverse the money and credit inflation. Money becomes tight, i.e., scarce; shaky businesses go bankrupt. The inflationary boom turns into a deflationary bust. With a reduced domestic money supply, prices, incomes and spending generally fall. Business becomes depressed.

Comparatively, foreign goods begin to look more expensive; imports decline. Domestic goods fall in price, exports increase, and the balance-of-trade and payments deficits reverse themselves. Gold (and/or silver) flows back into the nation to pay for increased exports.

The bankers remain cautious for a time and the depression continues until the unsustainable mistakes, distortions and excesses of the preceding inflationary boom have been liquidated. When the surviving businesses adjust their activities to the new situation and eventually get their financial affairs on a sounder footing, they become more creditworthy. The way is now paved for the cycle to begin again, whenever the bankers again become overconfident.

The cycle, of course, could not be repeated if the banks were denied the legal privilege of creating fictitious credits (loans) on their books.

The Austrian Explanation

The Ricardian or classical explanation of the "business cycle" as it is presented above has been well understood by

economists since the days of Adam Smith and the founding of
the United States. It remained for the Austrian School
economists, beginning early in the 20th century, to explain
that the classical theory of the business cycle — while correct
— was incomplete; that it did not nearly explain all of the
damage caused by periodic expansions and contractions of
money and credit.

A complete business cycle theory must explain two recurring
events not covered by classical theory. Why do large numbers
of businesses — even well-managed ones — suddenly and in
unison suffer heavy losses? And why in the past has recession
often hit hardest in capital goods industries?

The first complete explanation based upon a fully developed
theory was the work of the late Ludwig von Mises. He first
presented his monetary theory of business cycles in the German language edition of his *Theory of Money and Credit* in
1912. Mises elaborated and refined his theory in lectures at the
University of Vienna during the 1920s and published the fully
developed theory in an expanded version of the earlier work in
1928. It was first brought to the English-speaking world by his
student Friedrich Hayek in the early 1930s, in lectures at the
London School of Economics, and later elaborated and
published in a 1934 English-language edition of Mises' 1928
book, and in two of Hayek's early books: *Monetary Theory
and the Trade Cycle* and *Prices and Production*.

Briefly, building on the Ricardian theory, these Austrian
economists explained that the cycle affects various sectors and
participants in the economy unevenly at any point in time and
differently at different times in the course of a cycle. They first
demonstrated that in the absence of artificial money and
credit expansions in an otherwise free economy, the price
signals given by consumers to various producers would keep
each of their levels of production (and their necessary borrowing) closely in line with the true needs and wants of their own
customers. This would be so because, with no artificial new
buying power coming into the system, the available money
used to bid up the prices of goods in relatively scarce supply
would necessarily come from money withdrawn from bidding
for other goods in relative oversupply.

Thus, economic activity is well regulated by the competitive price system, which allocates profit rewards to producers of goods for which customers' demands are increasing and withholds profits from producers of goods for which customers' demands are decreasing. Under these conditions, with free capital markets for both equity and debt, investment capital flows in increased amounts to the more profitable prospering industries and producers, and in decreased amounts (or not at all) to the less profitable declining industries and producers. Thereby the unencumbered free market also regulates the allocation of capital to adjust production to meet the changing wants of customers.

Taking these efficient adjustment processes in both the consumer goods markets and the capital markets together, it is obvious that in a free market economy — functioning with sound and therefore limited money and credit — neither a boom nor a bust could occur in the overall economy.

However, in an economy saddled with fractional-reserve commercial banks guaranteed against failure by a central bank willing to buy debt securities from their portfolios, and further, to extend them credit at below market interest rates (with money the central bank creates out of nothing) the market restraints are replaced by opposite forces.

Banks have every incentive to expand their loans and virtually no disincentive to doing so. They act accordingly, and offer loans at interest rates much lower than they would be otherwise. The lower rates, of course, attract a much higher demand for loans than would otherwise occur, triggering and giving momentum to the money and credit expansion, i.e., to the inflation.

Then the Austrians explained more precisely what happens when artificial injections of new money and credit enter the economy. First of all, the new money — like an increased supply of anything else — tends to keep the cost of borrowing money (interest rates) down, below where it would be otherwise. (It does so, however, only as long as the public's inflationary expectations lag behind the true state of affairs.)

Immediately thereafter, businessmen in all industries — but especially capital-intensive ones with long lead times, where interest is a major part of costs — compare their current profit expectations with a reduced cost of borrowing, and are thereby encouraged to borrow and expand their productive facilities. Each of them interprets the newly favorable differential to mean — in effect — that his customers' wants are increasing relative to those of other producers. But, of course, for most of them it is a false signal which encourages malinvestments of capital. The mistaken ones who used the cheap money to invest in uneconomic expansion will later suffer, when they discover that their increased goods production (utilizing increased capital facilities financed by borrowing) can only be sold at reduced distress prices and hence at a lowered profit — often below their cost of borrowing — or at a loss. Further, with this result, their borrowing needs are involuntarily increased and, depending on the then availability of credit, they may be forced into bankruptcy — all because of the false signal.

Even those businessmen who, in fact, were enjoying relatively increased demand from their customers, are deceived by artificially low interest rates and encouraged to overexpand. The results for them are excess inventory, stretch-outs in capital projects, increased costs and lower-than-expected profits.

Still further, the Austrians explain that the impact of money and credit expansion — and of contraction or moderation — is much different for some industries and particular businessmen (and consumers) than it is for others.

Artificially created amounts of new money and credit do not simultaneously go out to everyone. Some necessarily get it first. Those who do, use this money for purchases or investments at lower prices than will be paid by those who receive it in later exchanges — after prices have been bid up.

Where the money and credit inflation is orchestrated by a central bank financing a central government's deficit spending — as in recent decades — most of the new money goes first to government, then to government employees, subsidy-beneficiaries and suppliers. They are the ones who benefit from inflation, to virtually everyone else's detriment. Simultaneously the new money goes to the commercial banks who purchase government debt securities, who also carry the accounts of the government and of those receiving payments from government.

Next in line are those who do business with the foregoing primary inflation beneficiaries; they pay higher prices than the first recipients but they, in turn, pay less and get more than those still later in the inflation stream, and so on.

Those at the end of the line, private enterprises and their employees doing business with other private enterprises, are the ones most victimized by money and credit inflation. They and their customers suffer the most, not only because they pay the highest prices but also because they are most damaged by the false signals and distortions caused by inflation — especially wildly gyrating nominal interest rates.

In the absence of inflation, interest rates would vary only moderately, within a range of perhaps 3 to 4 percent. Small changes over time reflect changes in the demands, i.e., the preferences on the part of both producers and consumers, for goods in the present versus goods in the future. Artificially low interest rates motivate businessmen to increase their investments in plant and equipment; simultaneously, they discourage savings on the part of the public and encourage consumption.

In general, consumers willing to borrow for consumption are expressing a preference for present goods versus future goods that is more intense than that of consumers who, on balance, are saving present income for future use. The competitive interplay between their borrowing and saving tends to move interest rates up or down moderately and occasionally to reflect gradual changes in the public's net time preferences over a period.

At higher rates more are encouraged to save; at lower rates more are encouraged to borrow. In the early stages of higher rates of inflation with higher nominal interest rates, saving is encouraged by interest rates substantially above the perceived rate of money depreciation (i.e., the overall rate of price increases). Later, however, when inflationary expectations race ahead, when interest rates are less than the generally perceived rate of money depreciation, overspending, overborrowing and overconsumption are encouraged.

The resulting consumer goods boom, in conjunction with in-

duced low interest rates in real terms, creates havoc in producer   industries and in business planning generally. In
response to soaring retail demand, retailers' orders to
wholesalers soar and, in turn, orders to manufacturers and
builders soar. They respond with plans and orders for expanded facilities and equipment. With leveraged effect, a capital
goods boom ensues.

The long-range planning, scheduling, and lead time for
capital-goods projects, involving massive borrowing, makes
credit less available to already overextended consumers. By the
time the buildings and capital equipment are completed, and
production from them begins, the consumer boom has run out
of steam. As consumer demand falls inventories begin to pile
up. Retail, wholesale and manufacturer orders are cancelled.
Production is cut back; capital goods orders are postponed or
cancelled. Facilities are closed and employees are laid off. The
unemployed and those fearing unemployment buy less. Consumer demand falls even more. Everyone has liquidity problems. Business profits nosedive. In short, the earlier credit
boom causes a depression.

The depression reduces incomes generally — including the
tax revenues of the federal government, while government expenditures for unemployment compensation and other sub-
sidies increase. The government deficit therefore grows
mightily at the very time both consumers and industry generally are squeezed financially. Government borrowing thus
crowds out private borrowers in the money market. Marginal
enterprises are unable to obtain credit and cannot survive;
bankruptcies increase. Even some large corporations require
government and/or central bank bail-outs to avoid bankruptcy.

At this juncture, what the federal government should do is
to slash its spending drastically and allow the depression to
liquidate all the accumulated malinvestments generally and
the over-production of capital goods in particular — and to
liquidate, therefore, the marginal firms involved. Economist
and historian Murray Rothbard explains the position in the
following words:

    . . .The government must not try to inflate again, in order to
    get out of the depression. For even if their reinflation succeeds,

it will only sow greater trouble and more prolonged and renewed depression later on. . .*What the economy needs is not more consumption spending but more saving, in order to validate some of the excessive investments of the boom.* (Emphasis added.)

Thus, what the government should do, according to the Misesian analysis of the depression, is absolutely nothing. . . Anything it does will delay and obstruct the adjustment process of the market; the less it does, the more rapidly will the market adjustment process do its work, and sound economic recovery ensue.

The Misesian prescription is thus the exact opposite of the Keynesian: It is for the government to keep absolute hands-off the economy, and to confine itself to stopping its own inflation, and to cutting its own budget.*

But, as we have seen — for reasons given in the preceding chapters — the federal colossus will not listen to a Mises, a Rothbard, nor a Smith.

Early in 1981 the floodgates of inflation will be wide open again, as they were in 1975 — only more so. Will the government succeed in "boosting the economy out of recession" one more time? Probably, but at the cost of a new surge in record high double-digit inflation in 1982 and the danger of imminent hyperinflation. Fear of this will probably be the excuse for imposition of wage and price controls — which, as described previously, would not solve the problem. But, at the expense of shackling the economy and enslaving the private population, it might enable the government to engineer one more cycle.

In the final cycle, still ahead of us, the attempt will fail and the result will be astronomically soaring prices and continued depression — in short, hyperinflation.

Capital Formation Under Attack

Saving, capital formation, by anyone in a society, benefits everyone in the society by increasing overall productive capacity and efficiency, thereby making more consumption

*Murray N. Rothbard, *Economic Depressions, Causes and Cures* (Constitutional Alliance, Inc., Lansing, Michigan, 1969), pp.18-26.

goods available to the total market at lower prices. The capitalist, by definition — whether he intends it to be so or not — is the greatest benefactor to his fellow men. Capital formation, as the late Dr. F.A. Harper put it, is "the greatest charity of all."

The opposite is equally true: capital consumption (or even worse, capital destruction) by anyone in a society is a detriment to everyone in the society because it decreases overall productive capacity and efficiency, thereby making fewer consumption goods available to the total market, and at higher prices. The anti-capitalist, by definition — whether he intends it to be so or not — is the greatest detractor to his fellow men. The greatest destroyer of capital, the greatest anti-capitalist, and therefore the greatest detractor to mankind is the state — particularly, but not only, in wartime.

During wartime the state's capability to destroy capital is at a maximum. During a prolonged inflation the state's ability to cause overall consumption of capital is maximized. Further, prolonged inflation grotesquely distorts market feedback and causes massive misallocations of capital, culminating in a severe shortage of capital where it is most needed (generally, in the consumption-goods industries) and a surplus of capital where it is not needed (generally, in the capital-goods industries) with the whole inflation matrix ending in an inflationary depression, which is where the world is headed today.

The U.S. federal state, following decades of prolonged war, inflation and rampant regulation, has directly and indirectly caused more misallocation, more destruction and more consumption of capital — and today is suffering a greater shortage of capital — than any nation in history. Principally, the attack on capital has centered on the corporation, because: (1) corporate retained earnings and paid-out earnings (dividends) together constitute the largest single source of funds for capital formation in modern society; and (2) corporations, particularly large publicly held ones, are easy "stationary targets" completely subject to every whim of the state (e.g., double taxation, taxation of phantom profits, inadequate depreciation allowances, forced capital expenditures for uneconomic, often destructive, decreed purposes and, generally, heavy-handed and uneven regulations of every imaginable sort).

If business is to expand at a rate providing ample jobs and rising living standards for all workers there must be sufficient investment in plants and equipment. And whether the money will be there in the coming decade is doubtful in light of the trends of recent decades. Before anyone decides to save and invest in producing capital goods he must decide whether the ultimate value of the investment to him is worth the sacrifice of leisure or immediate consumer goods. Whether he gives up *present* goods to acquire *future* goods depends on his subjective time-preference value scale, on his confidence in the future, and on his confidence in the future value of his money.

The continuous depreciation of the dollar through inflation simultaneously discourages saving and encourages consumption. In the last half-century, the United States has become a *consumer*-oriented rather than a *producer*-oriented society. Increased government "services," welfare and wealth-redistributing programs are examples of this trend. The U.S. state now has an economy whose tax structure and inflationist policies discourage savings and capital investment. There is little understanding of and only reluctant acceptance of the process by which business finances the nation's future. And the citadel of capitalism, the United States, has fallen far behind other nations in the percentage of total production that is allotted to capital investment.

Two major effects of long-continued inflation, as explained in the preceding sections, are the misallocation and consumption of capital and the consequent inflationary (or deflationary) depression. A third major effect is a massive, inequitable and destructive redistribution of wealth. These overall effects are accompanied by myriad other distortions which deepen and worsen the overall economic malaise.

The International Trade War

Few people are aware of the vast multitude and extent of the global array of trade barriers that have been erected in the past two decades. The principal reason for this, I suppose, is that, in news releases concerning the legislative and administrative acts of governments that affect world trade, their decrees are never *called* trade barriers. Universally they are called "voluntary" restraint agreements or are otherwise euphemistically titled to suit the author's *intended* purposes. Fewer people still — especially few in official posts — understand the *actual* effects of these restraints, duties, quotas, ceilings, floors and other regulations and controls. They are *always* damaging to the citizens of *both* of the affected nations.

Inflation distorts trade and creates a fertile environment for trade wars. Both tend to escalate, to stifle production, depress business and trade, and, long-continued, to lead to shooting wars. As Frederic Bastiat observed 130 years ago: "When goods do not cross borders, armies will."

The unprecedented world prosperity we enjoyed in the two decades following World War II was very largely a direct consequence of the dramatic increase in world trade — spreading the benefits of specialization and the division of labor across nation-state borders and creating a "world market economy" to a degree that had never existed before. This great expansion of world trade was made possible because of three interrelated and complementary conditions: (1) stable exchange rates, (2) negotiated reductions in tariffs and other trade restrictions, (3) the rise of multi-national manufacturing and trading companies.

Today all three of these essential conditions of continued world prosperity are under political attack. Today we have floating exchange rates, which are frequently subject to wide fluctuations. Trade barriers, far from being reduced, are proliferating as interest groups seek to protect their ailing industries from foreign competition. And there is a concerted and growing effort by governments to restrict and control the operations of multinational companies.

Because of these trends we must expect, without perhaps knowing the exact extent and timing, that the world economy is headed into a period of decline: a period that will be prefaced by a recession which, given a continuation of the political propensities that are evident today, will stretch into a world-wide inflationary depression, the likes of which the world has never seen.

Massive Wealth Redistribution

Of the three major means by which modern states redistribute income and wealth (income taxes, welfare spending and monetary inflation), inflation is by far the least understood and the most damaging. Taxes can be seen; they can be avoided, evaded and rebelled against. Welfare spending can be seen — it's in the budget — and its results can be seen and criticized by any astute observer. Inflation, on the other hand cannot even be seen, much less understood, by 99 percent of its victims; even its results, until they become extreme, are little noticed by most people — yet it robs them more capriciously and more ruthlessly than taxes; it takes the most from those least able to pay and least able to protect themselves.

Those who suffer most are the self-reliant poor, the subsistence wage earners and the retired, living on a slow-to-adjust or fixed income. They have no way to protect themselves as their incomes, in real terms, are eroded by more and more inflation. No matter how self-reliant and independent they would like to be, they are driven first to choose between deprivation and hunger *or* joining the welfare rolls — and, finally, as accelerating double-digit inflation outpaces increases in their welfare checks, they will have no choice. They will get poorer, and hungrier.

Increasingly, as this process continues, a small but growing percentage of the able-bodied poor are discovering a third alternative — they are turning more and more to vice and crime to supplement the diminishing value of their welfare incomes. As inflation accelerates, so will the incidence of vice, crime and violence accelerate, particularly in large cities.

Inflation's "benefits" go principally to the largest, most opulent of all institutions — the state (and its lackeys). Secondarily, benefits flow to those clever enough to turn the effects of inflation to their own advantage. An individual's only defense is his wits.

Those who are debtors in the dying currency win; those who are creditors lose. Who are these debtors (winners) and creditors (losers)?

The biggest debtor of all, of course, is the federal state. And, the biggest class of creditors are the lower and middle class wage and salary earners who buy and hold U.S. Treasury bonds and notes, either directly and/or through their pension plans and life insurance. This process, along with the graduated income tax, is destroying the American middle class — upon whom, more than any other, an industrial society depends for prosperity and progress.

Each year since 1970, double-digit inflation has pushed most middle class *nominal* (dollar) incomes up and moved these earners into a higher tax bracket while, overall, their *real* (purchasing power) income has declined. At the same time, double-digit inflation depreciates the real value of their savings, pensions and life insurance.

By this surreptitious process, annually increasing slices of income *and* wealth are taken from wage and salary earners by the state to sustain its growth and to subsidize a burgeoning multitude of non-producing welfare recipients. As always, the top earners and the very wealthy find ways, legal or otherwise, to escape being bled by either taxes or inflation. Thus, through these and other processes (e.g., discriminatory decrees and regulations) the Washington super-state is shrinking both the size and, more so, the resources of the middle class, while directly subsidizing the growth of the lowest (welfare) class and, perhaps less directly, facilitating the further enrichment of the already wealthy.

Inflation destroys conventional investments

CHAPTER SEVEN

Inflation's Effect on Conventional Investments

Inflation destroys investment funds by reducing their purchasing power. If the inflationary process is only partly completed, investment funds may be merely crippled. If the inflationary process is carried through to completion, the value of investment funds may be destroyed.

Inflation causes rising prices. This makes money less valuable. If an investor has to pay twice as much for goods and services, his investments are worth only half as much. He is in the same position as he would have been if the price level had remained unchanged and he had lost half his property. The value of investment funds depends on their purchasing power. Inflation, by causing higher prices, reduces or destroys purchasing power.

The investment problem presented by the possibility of inflation is extremely difficult for most investors. Inflation is deceptive because it is a slow process. Its effects seem slight at first. Its progress is usually punctuated by temporary halts which deceive many into believing that the inflation is ended.

—E.W. Axe & Co., Inc.
Inflation and the Investor

The longer inflation continues, the more damaging it is for conventional investments and conventional institutions. The damage is not limited to the very substantial erosion of the dollar value of most such investments over long periods. Equally damaging, and even more difficult to deal with, is the extreme price volatility it introduces into all markets; a factor that very few professional fund managers and still fewer among the investing public, are able to cope with over any period — short or long.

To do so successfully requires a complete reorientation of

one's thinking about investment values, and an entirely different set of talents than is possessed by the vast majority of
adults today, who learned their money management rules and
methods in the fifties and sixties, who still think in dollar terms
— and who, for the most part, were completely confused in
the seventies.

Those who cannot adapt will find the 1980s more confusing,
and not just damaging but disastrous; especially those who
have large amounts of their capital in bonds, savings accounts,
pensions, insurance and other dollar-denominated positions.

Dollar-Denominated Investments

Bonds

In an accelerating inflation, bonds are guaranteed losers
over any period of more than a few months because the value
of the fixed-dollar principal amount depreciates annually
more than the interest earnings, and the gap accelerates. Further, adding insult to injury, the government exacts a tax on
the nominal interest. In a hyperinflation, the financial
markets break down and bonds become worthless.*

---

*An indication that this could happen sooner than most would expect ap-
peared in a news item from the *Miami Herald* of February 10, 1980:

"NEW YORK — (AP) — Panic struck the bond markets for a while last
week, and the chaos that followed cost taxpayers millions of dollars in record
interest rates paid on Treasury borrowing.

"Prices dropped sharply early in the week and many firms that normally
offer price quotations on bonds were afraid to do so.

'There are no market-makers,' said William Gibson, an economist at
Smith Barney, Harris Upham & Co., 'Any change in sentiment tends to be
greatly magnified. What would have been a quarter-point change becomes
two points.'

"The result was huge swings in prices — most of them down. At the lows,
Triple-A rated telephone company bonds were yielding more than 13 percent
and 30-year Treasury bonds moved to almost 12 percent, both unprecedented levels."

Savings Accounts and Pensions

Savings accounts too are guaranteed losers for the same reasons. Their only advantage, compared to bonds, is that they are liquid at par, i.e., you can withdraw your cash and spend it or invest the proceeds in some appreciating tangible assets (excepting some pension funds). How the loss of purchasing power in dollar-denominated retirement funds, due to inflation at current rates, impoverishes old people is well illustrated by the following example:

Let's take the case of a person who retires early, say at age 60. The family owns its house outright; the husband has a company pension plan that pays him $600 a month. He has $100,000 in savings, divided between bonds, stocks and term deposits. Normally, the family would have little to worry about. It could supplement its $600-a-month pension from its investment income to give it $1,200 monthly. But statistics (and more relevantly, recent experience) indicate that the dollar has lost half of its value in the past ten years. Project this family situation ten years into the future and assume a similar rate of price increase. Now their situation is dramatically different. Their monthly real purchasing power in terms of what it will buy *today* is only $300 from the pension and $300 from their investments. And their capital has shrunk (in today's purchasing power) to only $50,000.

A more realistic assumption is that prices will increase faster in the next ten years. Assume prices are three times higher in ten years than they are today. The family will have the equivalent of only $400 a month income while the $100,000 savings will be worth only $33,000 in today's purchasing power.

Although the above example, of course, probably doesn't fit any individual exactly, there will be many who are in a somewhat similar situation or can see how the principles apply to his or her situation. The big objection amongst the unsophisticated is the belief that you must not eat into your principal but live off the interest alone. Of course, if you try to do this today, *while you live off the interest, the state lives off your principal.* Further, the state continues to live off the principal until the interest payment you receive will no longer buy enough to live at all.

The individual today must think in terms of the total purchasing power of his assets. He must ask himself what inflation is doing to his overall real wealth.*

The actual loss in purchasing power is greater than the official Consumer Price Index indicates, particularly for basic necessities.

The cost of food, housing, energy and health care rose 17.6 percent during 1979, by far the biggest jump of the decade, according to the National Center for Economic Alternatives.

Based on the Labor Department's Consumer Price Index, the group noted that during 1979 energy prices rose 37.4 percent, the price of shelter 17.4 percent, food 10.2 percent and medical care 10.1 percent.

The group's most striking finding — not clearly spelled out in government reports — was that there has been a virtual explosion in prices of necessities during the last four years. They rose 3.7 percent in 1976, 8.3 percent in 1977, 10.8 percent in 1978 and 17.6 percent last year. For the decade of the 1970s as a whole, the price of basic necessities rose 129 percent.

Insurance

In periods of extreme and accelerating inflation, life insurance, like bonds, cannot be considered an investment at all. Inflation makes long-term economic calculation difficult and very imprecise; high and accelerating rates of inflation make long-range dollar financial planning impossible.

Life insurance benefit amounts that might be appropriate today are only half enough in only four years at a dollar depreciation rate of 16 percent, one-third enough in six years, one-quarter in eight. Further, even if one's guess about the future average rate of dollar depreciation turns out to be close, at rates in the double-digit range, one cannot compensate by simply buying two, three or four times the presently required

*"Coping With Inflation — The Income Fallacy," by Lindsay B. Semple which appeared in the November 16, 1978 issue of *World Market Perspective*. Mr. Semple, a contributing editor to *World Market Perspective*, is a financial consultant who specializes in retirement planning; he is located in Vancouver, British Columbia.

principal amount without facing prohibitively high premium payments in current dollars. Still further, on the more realistic assumption that the recent year-to-year trend of successively higher double-digit dollar depreciation rates continues, then the possibility of any sensible use of dollar-denominated insurance for more than one or two years vanishes completely.

Finally, even such limited use is hazardous because as the trend to increasing double-digit inflation rates continues, the viability of various insurance companies and the industry as a whole is greatly impaired. Companies whose investment portfolios contain a high percentage of bonds (most of them) will see the value and liquidity of their portfolios plunge and their solvency threatened as increasing numbers of policy holders cash in their policies and abandon the use of insurance for the reasons discussed in the preceding paragraph.

Land

Farmland appreciates more than most other things in an accelerating inflation, and, in general, city and suburban land appreciates less.

City property values generally tend to lag the overall rate of price escalation for two basic reasons: (1) They are more directly affected by depressed business conditions, and (2) The ever-present danger exists of a municipal *or* federal imposition of rent controls (ceilings) while taxes, maintenance and other ownership costs are soaring. This danger is especially acute in the case of apartments and other residential rental properties.

Commodities

Commodities generally rise in price more than the rise in the overall price level. Metals, especially those of high unit value, which are diminishing, non-renewable resources important to industry and war, and which can be stored for long periods at low cost are far better inflation hedges than perishables. A note of caution is in order on strategic and rare metals, concerning the illiquidity of the markets for these metals and the wide spreads between dealers' buying and selling quotations.

All commodities, especially those traded on American futures markets, are subject to wide and erratic price movements, up and down, in periods of a year or less. For this reason, anyone who is not thoroughly knowledgeable on all relevant market and industry factors affecting a particular commodity *and* who is not also professionally qualified as a commodity trader, should not attempt to trade commodities personally. Readers who are not so qualified who insist on trading in spite of this warning should seek out a thoroughly qualified professional account manager with a proven record over a period of at least five years and let him manage their trading.*

Each commodity, of course, has to be studied separately and individually considered at any given time. Further, any time that a move into or out of a commodity position is being contemplated, one must assess the current overall inflationary trends and their expected future impact on commodities generally. Still further, mass psychology — greed, fear and other emotional elements — of market participants must be considered in the timing of one's moves.**

Several independent studies have demonstrated that 95 percent of the novices who trade in the commodities futures markets lose their capital, and soon leave the markets poorer but wiser. The winners are the professional traders, who comprise about 20 percent of those in these markets at any given time, and the brokers who collect their commissions no matter which way the markets move. For those readers who, in spite of these dire statistics, are nevertheless considering commodities futures trading, probably the best outlay they could possibly make beforehand would be to purchase a simple but effective teaching game called "Limit Up," invented by

*One such firm that I know is CPISA, Apartado 136, Centro Colon, San Jose, Costa Rica.

**For a thorough discussion of commodity markets, see the *World Market Perspective* issues of February 1979 ("Commodity Market Losers and Winners") and August 1979 ("An Economic Approach to Commodity Investing").

banker Nicholas Platt. The game simulates actual trading very
well. Most of those who play it lose the $12,500 of scrip they
start with.*

Common Stocks

The short-term effects of inflation on the stock market in
general or on any particular stock at any given time are impossible to predict. Inflation makes all markets extremely
volatile, up and down, in the short run, and generally up over
a period of years. Thus, one may make a good choice at the
wrong time and lose, or a wrong choice at the right time and
win — for a time at least.

In real value terms, the prices of most shares tend to decline
because most nominal business profits are fictitious. Amounts
set aside for depreciation are usually insufficient. Replacement
costs for both inventory and equipment soar, while depreciation allowable under the tax laws is based on past costs and is
therefore insufficient to cover future replacement costs. The
fact that reported profits are largely fictitious causes companies to pay income taxes when there is no real income, and
declare dividends while actually working at a loss.

In general, inflation causes massive distortions, misallocation of resources, mounting uncertainties and is bad for
business and therefore bad for share values, especially so in
real (purchasing) value terms. In order to gain in the stock
markets in an accelerating inflation one must choose the right
stocks, viewed in the long run, *and* the right time to buy,
viewed in the short and intermediate term.

Stock Selection Criteria

As a class, the shares of companies, especially natural
resource companies, which meet the following criteria will
fare best in a period of accelerating inflation. Their balance
sheets should show a heavy concentration of real assets (such as

*The game can be ordered by mail ($45 plus $3.50 handling) from Limit Up,
P.O. Box 1200, New York N.Y. 10028.

natural resources,* modern capital-intensive manufacturing
facilities, etc.), with a high percentage of long-term debt in
their capitalization. And, they should have competent
(inflation-conscious) management. This means, for example,
that their inventory cost accounting is done on a last-in, first-
out basis; they own rather than lease their major capital
equipment; and they either have or plan soon to adopt "inflation accounting," also called current cost accounting, whereby
assets are revalued each reporting period to reflect their
replacement cost, and, of course, with commensurate increases in earnings retained to fund replacement. Unfortunately, few companies today can meet these criteria.

If you must invest in common stocks, avoid the high-flyer
speculative stocks; search for shares with good price/earnings
ratios, below eight, and/or price/dividend ratios, below twenty. *Above all, select shares that are cheap in relation to the
book value of real assets.* Only buy a stock that looks good for
the next five years — but be prepared to sell it anytime after
one year if it no longer meets the foregoing criteria and/or any
time the general economic conditions no longer meet the
criteria that are given below.

Timing Criteria

As to timing of stock purchases, I have no dependable short-
term advice — and, as a matter of historical fact, neither does
anyone else. As to intermediate-term timing, buy your carefu-
ly selected shares, if you can, in a non-presidential election
year** in which *most* of the following conditions prevail, approximately at least:

1.   It is soon after an apparent recession bottom, such as
     occurred in 1954, '58, '61, '71 and '75;
2.   It is about three years after a stock market top;

*Especially mining companies heavy in ownership of precious metal deposits
that are only marginally profitable at recent metal prices. The same rationale, however, also applies to oil and coal producers, forest products, etc.

**The "summer rally" preceding each of the last four elections was a good
time to sell.

3. The share indices are at least 20 percent, and preferably 30 percent, below their last peak;
4. Interest rates have trended down in the preceding year and are at least 30 percent below their last peak;
5. Money is easy; the Fed is doing its best to push interest rates even lower and to increase the rate of increase in money supply inflation, while corporate and banking liquidity is much improved from year-ago levels;
6. Price/earnings ratios for stocks generally are below 12 and price/dividend ratios are near or below 25;
7. Virtually everyone is pessimistic on the outlook for business, the economy and the stock market.

These criteria are not as complicated or difficult as they may seem at a glance because they all tend to happen together, though perhaps not at the precise numbers I have indicated and not necessarily at exactly the same time. One should be satisfied if four or five come together in a given quarter, while another one or two are near or approaching the indicated levels.

It is obvious that 1980, by the above criteria, is not a year to buy common stocks generally. It further appears, to me at least, that with the exception of some natural resource and high technology companies, we will probably not find a good year for common stocks generally until the world's problem with unsound money is solved, and not before sometime around the mid-1980s at the earliest in any case.

The Eight Tee's for capital survival

CHAPTER EIGHT

Capital Survival Strategy

Let every man divide his money into three parts, and invest a third in land, a third in business, and a third let him keep by him in reserve.

— Hebrew Proverb

Traditional rules of money management — given unsound, depreciating paper money — lead to the incremental destruction of one's principal at rates exceeding dividend and interest income rates — and, ultimately, to the destruction of most of one's capital. During a runaway inflation, the investor's primary concern must be the preservation of his capital. With conventional avenues becoming guaranteed losers, he must seek new investments, evaluating them according to new criteria.

Investment Guidelines for a Runaway Inflation

There are three essential general rules for preserving capital in an accelerating inflation.

1. *Own real assets* (e.g., precious metals). Own tangible, physical, preferably portable economic goods, not dollar-amount instruments or accounts.

2. *Owe "money" debts* (to have inflation working for you). Use borrowed paper dollars (or other currencies*) to increase total holdings of real assets.

*To the extent that it is necessary or prudent to own any currency or currency-denominated asset, you should own a strengthening currency — and you should *owe* money debts denominated in a weakening currency or currencies.

97

3. *Stay liquid* (i.e., stay solvent). Don't over-borrow. Over-
    borrowing or over-leveraging is not a means of preserving
    your capital — it is gambling. The volatility of today's
    markets makes the risks involved in gambling (for in-
    stance, in futures markets) too great to be borne except by
    professional traders.

These three rules are primary and universal but they do not
give any clues as to *what* real assets one should own for maximum security. I will attempt to compensate for that lack, in
part at least, by introducing eight compatible guidelines
which I believe will be helpful to everyone selecting specific
investments for an overall investment program. I call these the
Eight Tee's, for ease in remembering.

The Eight Tee's for the Eighties

The first one is Safe*ty*, the others are Liquidi*ty*, Tangibili*ty*,
Profitabili*ty*, Leverageabili*ty*, Stabili*ty*, Diversi*ty* and
Suitabili*ty*. I will define each of these with a short comment.

(1) *Safety:* This doesn't need much comment; it should
    always be the first consideration for any investor. It will
    not be found in an asset that is continually depreciating,
    as any dollar-denominated asset is, because the rate of
    monetary depreciation is higher than the interest rate on
    most debt instruments and all bank accounts.

(2) *Liquidity:* The investment one should be seeking is in
    something that is regularly and widely traded, preferably
    on a daily basis and in many different markets.

(3) *Tangibility:* It must have a value in and of itself, one not
    dependent upon the "full faith and credit" of any par-
    ticular government. Given the political, monetary and
    economic outlook in the world today, the "full faith and
    credit" of the government of the United States and that of
    the other major nation-states isn't worth the paper it is
    printed on.

(4) *Stability:* This refers not to the investment itself, but to
    the safety and permanence of the markets and the
    institutions involved in investing. (In the bear stock
    market of recent years, particularly in the low-volume,

300-point drop in 1974, many brokerage houses went under or were forced to merge, and a sizeable number have done so more recently.)

(5) *Profitability:* This is purposely ranked number five, since each of the first four has to do with preservation of capital — which should always be the prime consideration, at least for the major part of one's capital. Once you are satisfied that your capital is secure, *then* look to the profit potential of an investment.

(6) *Leverageability:* This is simply the use of margin and borrowed money to take the fullest advantage of price changes. When the other factors are present, I recommend the conservative use of margin to multiply the potential of both the real profitability from an economic standpoint, and the nominal profitability from an inflationary factor standpoint.

(7) *Diversity:* Economic and financial common sense call for asset diversification amongst several (but not too many) categories of assets. Political realities and prudence indicate that one's assets should be diversified geopolitically in at least two and preferably three national jurisdictions with the bulk of one's capital outside one's own nation of citizenship and/or residency.

(8) *Suitability:* One should consider one's own personal situation, objectives and perspective vis-a-vis the intended investment. Most people lose on short-term trades because they fail to do this. Long-term investments that feel comfortable are much better for most people.

These guidelines for investments in an inflationary depression are not the only ones that could be listed. I think, however, that they are the most important ones. They can be applied to any investment you may be considering.

Portfolio Management Rules

The key to using the three general rules given at the beginning of this chapter is to maintain a proper balance between all three, at all times, and the difficulty is that the second and third involve a trade-off.

For the very rich, this presents no problem, because their command of large and diverse holdings of real assets eases prudent management of debt and liquidity. For those of more modest wealth, the following rules should prove helpful. These apply to all investment markets.

1. Thoroughly study every discernable relevant factor, and the relationships between factors (e.g., supply and demand) before making any investment decision.
2. In all investment selections, take a long-term perspective; do not attempt to speculate short-term.
3. Always have economic reasons for your selections and timing; never buy or sell purely for tax considerations, and never act on emotions or tips.
4. Whenever your original reasons for buying are no longer operative, and the market price turns even a little against you, sell immediately "at market."
5. Buy "at market," i.e., don't use "limit" buy or sell orders, except when the market is extremely volatile or when the short-term trend is against you.
6. When you buy, immediately place a "stop-loss" order 8 percent to 10 percent below your buy price, and keep it — raise it but don't lower it. (If you get "stopped-out," stay out until the trend is again with you.)
7. Never meet a margin call; sell and wait until the trend is again clearly with you.
8. Buy soon after a bottom, sell and/or sell short soon after a top — never go against a trend.
9. Diversify among at least a half-dozen, but not more than ten, different investments, and, except for precious metals (which are in fact real cash), never risk more than 10 percent of your capital in any one commitment.
10. Hedge; at least 20 percent of your capital should be in investments that will do well if the markets go against your major holdings.
11. Keep a cash reserve of at least 10 percent of your investment capital for emergencies and in order to take advantage of sudden and unexpected bargains.
12. Maintain at least 40 percent equity in all hedge investments.
13. Steer clear of thinly margined futures contracts.

Investments for Capital Preservation

Using the Eight Tee's discussed previously, where should the investor put his money for maximum security? The investments offering the greatest security during a runaway inflationary period are the precious metals, collectibles and diamonds.

The *precious metals*, gold and silver especially, but also platinum in present circumstances, are the premier investments for everyone during the middle and late stages of a period of accelerating inflation, especially one that culminates in a hyperinflation. Gold and silver are the real money of the globe; in the later extreme phases of accelerating, runaway inflation their prices will reflect the depreciation of paper money more fully, more dependably and more instantaneously than will anything else. Platinum also tends generally to move in price with gold and silver in reaction to money inflation.

Collectibles are also sound inflation hedges for the knowledgeable, but with less liquidity than the precious metals. And *diamonds* offer great appreciation potential with the prospect of ever-decreasing supplies.

One further investment, the *Swiss franc*, warrants careful scrutiny. The franc has performed superbly in the past in dollar terms, and will, I believe, do so again in the second half of 1980 and in 1981.

Silver

The single best investment today, in my judgment, is silver. All the reasons are given in my book *Silver Profits in the Seventies*, and an updated summary is contained in a recent special report titled *Profits from Silver.**

Silver was one of the earliest metals known to man. The richest ores, including much native silver, originally lay right on the surface of the earth. Prior to the last century, some deposits could actually be found glistening in the sunlight

*ERC Publishing Company, 212-585 16th Street, West Vancouver, British Columbia, Canada.

(before men burned enough fossil fuels to pollute the air with sulfur). As long ago as 4000 B.C., silver was fashioned into ornaments, some of which were placed in the royal tombs of Chaldea; it was also the favorite ornamental metal for the Mesopotamians, Egyptians, Chinese, Persians and Greeks. It has served as money in more times and places than gold. From ancient times, it has been used for making mirrors and table utensils. Today, because of several unusual technical properties, silver has many new and vital uses, especially in photography and in electronics. It is today, more than ever, a very useful substance.

Table IV compares total production supply of silver from all sources and total demand for all uses of silver in recent years, for the world, excepting communist-dominated areas.

TABLE IV
World Silver Supply vs. Demand
(millions of ounces)

	1975	1976	1977	1978	1979
New production	240.1	246.6	267.4	265.0	271.0
All other sources*	195.3	209.4	149.2	154.5	131.7
From private inventories	(19.8)	(4.3)	20.1	14.1	30.1
Market Supply	415.6	451.7	436.7	433.5	432.8
Industrial uses	376.8	422.0	417.5	404.5	410.0
Coinage	38.8	29.7	19.2	29.0	22.8
Market Demand	415.6	451.7	436.7	433.5	432.8
Remaining private inventories (est.)	216.0	226.0	319.5	385.2	362.2

*From government inventories, from India and salvage recovered from photography, scrap silverware and scrap from industries other than refiners.
Source: Handy and Harman.

Fully 75 percent of silver mined worldwide is a byproduct of copper, lead and zinc mining. Only 25 percent comes from mines worked principally for the silver content of the ore. Even very large increases in the silver price therefore only influence the production of one-quarter of the mines.

The total amount of silver consumed for each of the major industrial uses is huge. Yet, excepting only sterlingware, the individual amount of silver used *per unit of manufacturers' products is minuscule*. But *that amount* is vital. And the cost of the silver used per unit of final product is, in virtually every instance, a small percentage of total production costs. The point is that silver is price inelastic on the demand side as well as on the supply side. A very large price increase will have very little effect on either silver's static supply or the growing demand for silver.

Further, with the more than 150 million ounce annual shortfall (nearly 162 million ounces in 1979) between new production and total consumption, the world is heavily dependent on (1) salvage recovery, which peaked out at 86.5 million ounces in 1979, and (2) remaining aboveground stocks, which according to Handy and Harman at 1979 yearend, totalled 362.2 million ounces.

The price of silver has risen more than 700 percent over its 1968 level. (See Chart 7 on page 105.) As existing aboveground supplies are depleted, the price will continue to rise in the 1980s and beyond, as far as anyone can see.

Gold

Gold has always been the principal money metal, valued for its beauty, utility and durability. Today, it is more highly prized than ever, and its value will continue to rise according to the decline of fiat paper currencies.

Gold is, however, particularly subject to short-term price fluctuations. Nation-states and their central banks hold about half of the globe's aboveground stores of gold, with which they can and do engineer extreme short-term price declines. And, as more than 95 percent of the gold mined in the past still exists, with most of it in bullion bar form, the globe's stores of gold are perhaps a hundred times larger than the annual world production of gold — and nearly a hundred times more potentially influential, on the supply side, to short-term price movements.

Industrial demand for and production supply of gold annually are about matched, although adverse political changes in either of the two principal producer nations (South Africa and the U.S.S.R.) could alter that balance.

However, private demand for gold is particularly sensitive to two factors: currency exchange-rate depreciation, and political instability. A worsening of either of these conditions will materially increase demand for gold.

Moreover, official government purchases of gold are increasing. Since 1978, IMF members' central banks have been permitted to purchase gold on the open market. The Less Developed Nations, too, are now permitted to make purchases of gold, rather than accepting paper from the IMF. And the enormous demand for gold in the Middle East, both by OPEC governments and by the ordinary citizen (in the form of gold jewelry) has noticeably boosted the total demand for gold.

Gold is a barometer of the value of fiat currencies. As fewer and fewer people have confidence in paper as a store of value, the price of gold will continue to rise.

Platinum

In a very short time, platinum has moved out of research and development laboratories and into the industrial complex as a valuable catalyst for many different processes in industry. It is widely used in the chemical, electrical and petroleum industries, as well as in the space industry as a catalyst for fuel cell power supplies and as a protective coating for space vehicle surfaces. All these industries are major suppliers both to other manufacturers and wholesalers generally, and to the aerospace/defense industry particularly.

The U.S. consumes about a third of world usage and produces less than one percent of its needs, importing 99 percent. For many years the biggest uses have been in the chemical, electrical and petroleum industries. Since the early 1970s, with the introduction of catalytic exhaust devices, the largest user in the U.S. and some other nations has been the automotive industry.

In a little over a decade, total industrial consumption of

Chart 7
Gold, Silver and Platinum $ Prices

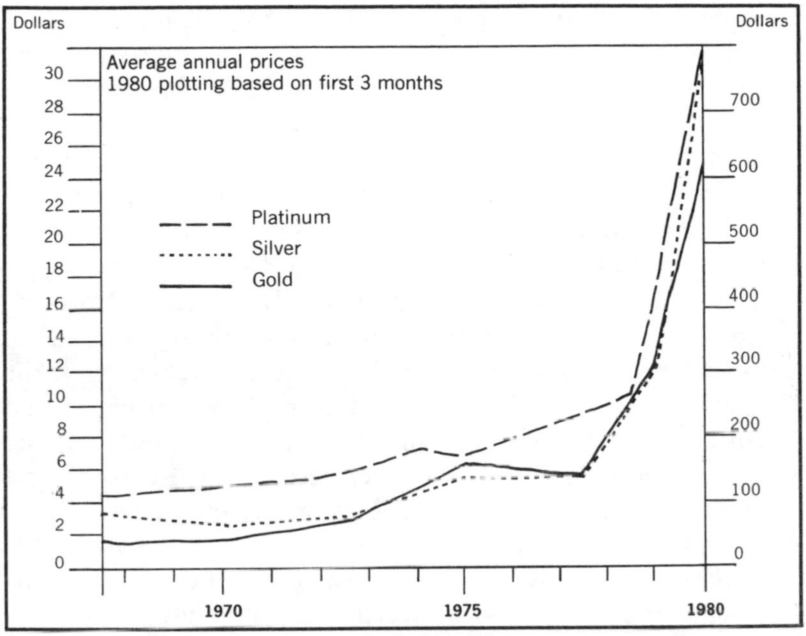

Dollars   Dollars

Average annual prices
1980 plotting based on first 3 months

30 —
28
26
24
22
20
18
16
14
12
10
8
6
4
2
0

700
600
500
400
300
200
100
0

– – – Platinum
.... Silver
——— Gold

1970   1975   1980

platinum has more than doubled. It has become potentially
more valuable in industry than gold on a per-ounce basis
because of its relatively greater scarcity coupled with its many
and varied uses, which depend upon platinum's numerous
unique chemical and physical attributes.

Since the beginning of recorded history, 3,000 million
ounces of gold have been mined, most of which still exist as
bullion in various bank vaults and private and government
stockpiles. By contrast, the total platinum mined to date is
only 35 million ounces, *85 times less than the total amount of
gold mined*, and each year virtually the entire new increment
of mine production is consumed by industry. Logically it appears that this must eventually be reflected, to some substantial degree, in its price relative to gold.

Platinum's price over a period of months is largely subject to
industrial supply and demand factors and over a period of
years to its cost of production, but it has also tended to move in

tandem with gold and silver in recent years as can be seen in Chart 7. If and when the U.S. begins its planned program of purchasing platinum to add to its current stockpile of 452,645 ounces, we can expect to see the price of platinum soar to new highs once again. The United States' stockpile objective, if the program becomes effective, would be for 1,314,000 ounces.

Most of the platinum imported into the United States comes from South Africa, which accounts for about 60 percent of world production; the U.S.S.R. is in second place (about 30 percent), with Canada a distant third (about 8 percent).

In his well-documented book, *The War on Gold*,* Antony Sutton concludes that a soon forthcoming military war, in the decades-long ideological war, will see either the Soviets or the U.S. invading South Africa, either directly or through hired pawn nations; the pretext will be to end apartheid, but the real object will be control of that "geographical freak's" vast mineral resources. Others, including myself, have earlier reached much the same conclusion.

If this conclusion is correct, and especially if the Soviets out-maneuver the U.S. in southern Africa, which now seems like-ly, the consequent absence of South African mineral exports from world trade would drive the prices of all of those minerals up almost instantly. The metal that would surge highest in price as a direct result, in my opinion, is platinum. Further, as one of the three principal precious metals, platinum in recent years has tended to follow gold and silver in price; it is thus a hedge against both war *and* inflation; even, perhaps, more so than gold because of the absence of any large stockpiles of platinum.

Collectibles

Fine art, antiques, rare stamps, vintage photographic prints, numismatic coins and other valuable collectibles do very well overall in an accelerating inflation. However, it is *essential* that one be expert, or at least have reliable expert advice, in selecting and accumulating collectibles. Further, most

*Published in 1977 by '76 Press, Seal Beach, CA 90740.

collectibles are *not liquid*, i.e., it may be impossible to find a buyer when you want to sell.

Numismatic coins are the best collectible choice for most people because: (1) good, reliable expert advice is readily and widely available; (2) prices are competitively established daily on the coin teletype network for most numismatic coins and less often but still frequently for rarer coins; and (3) they are the *most liquid* of all collectibles. They can be bought or sold at a fair price almost anytime, and almost anywhere.

Diamonds

The earth does not give up its hardest substance easily. In the last 3,000 years, only 230 tons of diamonds have been mined. To obtain even one rough diamond, anywhere from 50 to 250 tons of earth must be meticulously sifted.

Only three countries are responsible for 90 percent of all new production: South Africa, the U.S.S.R. and Brazil. (It is too early, given the information so far available, to comment intelligently on the prospects for the new Kimberly find in Australia.) The next important producers are the African states of Botswana, Angola and Zaire. It is noteworthy that few of these countries are politically stable. A war involving any of them would seriously disrupt new diamond production and further restrict the supply.

And even if these areas become trouble-free, the fact is that world supplies are running out. From 1947 to 1970 world diamond production steadily increased from 10 million carats to 50 million carats annually. Since then it has first remained stable and then declined to 47 million carats in 1976. Every outlook is for dwindling production in the future. Indeed, all presently known diamond reserves will be worked out in about 30 years.

Until very recently, however, diamonds would not have been a feasible investment to recommend to a large audience. One had to have either personal expert knowledge or direct advice from a reliable expert, in order to assess a particular diamond's value. Further, there was no general market to enable laymen to skirt the large mark-up price of dealers. Perhaps most importantly, the lack of a large market meant an absence of liquidity, i.e., an easy way to make a quick sale. However, in recent years, the increased popularity of investment diamonds and the corresponding increase in the numbers of dealers has improved liquidity quite substantially.

The Swiss Franc

Regarded in terms of land mass and population, Switzerland is a tiny nation. Yet, Swiss influence greatly over-reaches her national boundaries. This is particularly true in the financial world, where Switzerland is a giant and a model for others.

The Swiss franc has no peer among paper currencies. Since 1970, it has appreciated 282 percent against the dollar, 5 percent against a strong German mark (which has made a recent comeback), and over 400 percent against the chronically ill Italian lira.

This superb exhibition of strength stems from Switzerland's avoidance, between 1973 and 1979, of the currency-cheapening techniques of printing-press inflation.

Prior to 1973, the Swiss abided by the Bretton Woods system of fixed exchange rates even though Switzerland had never been a member of the International Monetary Fund. According to this system, the Swiss National Bank was obligated to buy, at a fixed franc price, all dollars unwanted by Swiss commercial banks. With the increasing supply of dollars in the late '60s, the dollar, then 4.37 francs (or 23 cents per franc), became more and more overvalued against other more conservatively managed currencies. The German mark, the Dutch guilder and the Swiss franc were undervalued. Thus, the burden of supporting the U.S. dollar fell on the central banks of those three countries.

This burden was heavy. The Swiss of necessity printed francs to pay for the unwanted dollars. While the U.S. still honored its dollar-redeemability commitment to other nations, the Swiss government could redeem some of these dollars for gold. However, the U.S., in danger of losing its entire official gold holdings, effectively suspended redeemability in 1968, doing so formally in August 1971. But to their own detriment, the Swiss continued to prop up the value of the

dollar for yet another year. The Swiss money supply ballooned, soaring 22 percent in 1971. This was clearly too much.
Beginning in 1972, the Swiss restricted their purchases of
dollars and froze their domestic monetary inflation rate.

On January 24, 1973, the Swiss stopped supporting the
Bretton Woods system altogether. One month later the entire
fixed exchange-rate setup collapsed. Since then, except for
1979, the franc's value has risen steadily.

For the past two years, however, the Swiss national money
managers have been in a dilemma. Until quite recently, they
attempted to contain the rise in the Swiss franc by heavy intervention in the foreign exchange markets, a reversion to their
pre-1973 policies. To carry out this intervention they issued
new Swiss francs, selling them in exchange for U.S. dollars.
This operation was less than a notable success from the Swiss
standpoint because it failed to stop the franc from making
higher highs against the dollar. During 1978 the franc's value
reached 67 cents, an increase of nearly 300 percent over its
1970 value. At the same time the new Swiss franc issues
ballooned the Swiss money supply by more than 17 percent.
This was a fundamental change from Swiss money-supply performance in the preceding five years, and contributed to the
decline of the franc to 56 cents in 1979.

What the Swiss (and the Germans, the Dutch, the Japanese
and others) should do now is what they should have been doing since August 1971; that is, instead of printing more of their
own currencies to buy depreciating dollars and thus weakening their own currencies in the longer term, in terms of purchasing value at least, they should (while freezing their dollar
balances at present levels) be using any available amounts of
their currencies to buy appreciating gold, the value reciprocal
of the dollar, and thus strengthening their own currencies.

If the Swiss wake up to this profoundly simple solution soon
and act upon it vigorously, the Swiss franc, in my judgement,
could be saved from the 1980s global hyperinflation. If they
are unwilling or unable to return to sound policies, their currency will suffer the same fate as other fiat national currencies. Sooner or later, everyone everywhere will catch on to the
fact that the national currency game is drawing to a close —
that all fiat currencies are doomed.

Indeed, action in the marketplaces in 1979, which I expect
to resume in the second half of 1980, suggests that this recognition *is* spreading; that a flight from all national currencies into
real values is developing and will gain momentum as the 1980s
unfold. In response to this recognition, market activity will
focus more and more on hard-asset tangibles — gold, silver,
platinum, diamonds, etc. — which will soar in price in terms
of all currencies.

Nevertheless, the outlook for 1980 and 1981 at least — bar-
ring greatly increased fears of war or actual war in central
Europe — is for the Swiss franc to strengthen markedly against
the dollar, though not against the precious metals.*

A Portfolio for Runaway Inflation

Considering the foregoing and the prospect that the next
surge in double-digit price increases may suddenly accelerate
into triple-digit hyperinflation, I recommend for most people
that at least 60 percent of total investment capital be in a hard-
money-oriented portfolio. Such a portfolio should consist principally of the following, in the order of their importance:

(a)   Silver bullion: 40 percent to 50 percent, in a Swiss bank;
(b)   Common silver coins: 5 percent to 10 percent in posses-
       sion;**

*The current outlook for silver, gold, platinum and the Swiss franc is
reported regularly in each monthly issue of *World Market Perspective*. (US
$96.00 annual subscription from ERC Publishing Company, 212-585 16th
Street, West Vancouver, British Columbia, Canada.)

**United States silver half-dollars, quarters and dimes minted prior to 1965
have a silver content of 90 percent. Bulk U.S. silver coins are a unique investment. They have the same appreciation potential as bullion because of their
metal content. In addition, upon a complete currency collapse, U.S. silver
coins will reappear as a standard medium of exchange in private markets at a
high multiple of their face value.

For this contingency, I recommend that each individual (or family) purchase one or two ($1,000 face amount) bags of silver coins from a reputable
domestic coin dealer, pay for them in full, take delivery and keep them in his
possession as an emergency reserve fund of real spending money which will
always buy food and other necessities at any time and under virtually any
circumstances.

(c) Gold bullion: 10 percent to 15 percent, in a Swiss bank;
(d) Platinum bars: 5 percent to 10 percent, in a Swiss bank;
(e) Gold coins: 10 percent to 15 percent, one-half in a Swiss bank, one-half in possession;*
(f) Diamonds: 5 percent to 10 percent;
(g) Cash or equivalent: 10 percent to 15 percent, three-quarters in a Swiss bank, one-quarter in possession; held in an appreciating currency.

These percentages are given in ranges and are only approximate because personal circumstances and preferences vary widely and must be taken into account individually by each investor. Further, whether hard-money investments should represent a major or minor portion of one's total portfolio also depends upon individual factors, particularly the magnitude of the total amount of one's financial assets. In general, the percent ranges given above are suitable for five-digit hard-money portfolios — smaller ones should favor coins more heavily; larger ones should favor bullion and currency deposits more heavily and should also include a larger proportion of diamonds. However, no one recommendation fits everyone, *and I suggest readers seek individual counsel and advice from a knowledgeable professional counselor.*

As a final word, using the Eight Tee's as a guide, there are also some dangerous traps to avoid. (1) The most serious trap is *having funds locked in fixed return instruments: bonds, term deposits, etc.* (2) Another serious trap to avoid is *being a lender against mortgages.* (3) Further, although equity markets may rise strongly on occasion, *the stock market will halt in its tracks and reverse its course each time double-digit inflation clearly reappears, and can be expected to drop precipitously in real value terms at the earliest obvious sign of hyperinflation.*

---

*This should be mostly common, low-premium "bullion"-type coins but could include some numismatic coins.

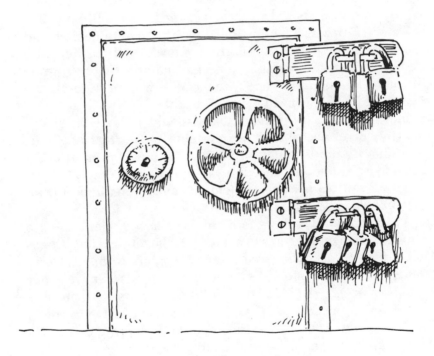

The right to privacy

CHAPTER NINE

Capital Protection: The Right to Privacy

. . .It is very easy to awaken resentment against people who not only have money, but also the boldness to send that money abroad via more or less legal channels, in order to protect it against all manner of domestic insecurity. And it is only a short step from there, to extend that resentment to the country and the banks which receive such money and which grant it not only asylum but also the kind of guarantee of safety represented by discretion and secrecy.

These thoughts, while probably not very popular, are nevertheless necessary to shake the dogmatic belief that "capital flight" is always something objectionable. In a world which, even when it calls itself "free," is subjecting the individual increasingly to the yoke of the state, it is vital that people and their means of existence — that is, capital — still have the chance to move about internationally and, when absolutely necessary, to escape the arbitrariness of government policy by means of secret back doors. This is probably one of the key reasons why, even under the most discouraging conditions, there is still some remnant of freedom left. . . .

—Wilhelm Röpke
The Bank in Our Time

Any listing of human rights becomes less complete and more prone to error in proportion to how specific it is. This is, I suppose, why the Declaration of Independence begins its listing with "among these (rights) are. . ." indicating the author's acknowledgment that the listing is not intended to be complete. The prime right is one's right to life, one's *own* life and no one else's. All other rights, and the delineation of whose is what, derive from this beginning.

Thus, that which is pro-life is a right and is moral and that which is anti-life is a usurpation and immoral. All human

113

rights — and which actions are right (moral) and which are wrong — can be logically derived from the prime right, the right to life.

The way in which the three traditionally listed rights are logically bound together was well expressed by Justice Sutherland as follows:

> The individual has three rights, equally sacred from arbitrary interference (from government): the right to life, the right to his liberty, the right to his property. These three rights are so bound together as to be essentially one right. To give a man his life, but to deny him his liberty, is to take from him all that makes life worth living. To give him his liberty, but to take from him the property which is the fruit and badge of his liberty, is to still leave him a slave.

The logical chain, from life to liberty to property, extends another step from property to privacy, i.e., the right to exclusivity in the enjoyment of one's own life, one's own liberty, and one's own property; privacy in brief is the right to be unmolested — the right to be let alone.* Without this right, each of the other three is compromised and vulnerable to destruction by an omnipotent state staffed by self-styled gods seeking to establish an omniscient state. They cannot succeed. But they can destroy what little freedom remains — and civilization — in the attempt.

In lawless nation-states today, producers have already lost their life-given right to "the fruit of their liberty"; it is *de jure*

---

*In 1890 Louis Brandeis and Samuel Warren wrote an article for the *Harvard Law Review* urging the creating of a legal right of privacy. New technological methods of snooping have made privacy an even more cherished value. Brandeis was on the Supreme Court in 1928 when it decided that police wire-tapping was not a "search" subject to constitutional restrictions, and in a great dissent he reiterated a passage from his 1890 article:

"The makers of the Constitution. . .sought to protect Americans in their beliefs, their thoughts, their emotions, and their sensations. They conferred, as against the Government, the right to be let alone — the most comprehensive of rights and the right most valued by all civilized men." (Justice Louis D. Brandeis, in *Olmstead vs. U.S.*, 1928.)

The Supreme Court since then has adopted the Brandeis dissent as the law on wire-tapping and, in general, declared privacy a value respected by the Constitution.

no longer their property. It belongs legally to the tax officials who allow producers to keep just enough for their sustenance, so they can continue to produce more to be taxed again. Through this they are enslaved and, by definition, have lost most of their property and much of their liberty.

The state's attack today is focused on the individual's enjoyment of his right to privacy, in an effort to further encroach upon liberty and property heretofore beyond the state's reach. In the statist view, privacy is a black market in liberty and a barrier to establishing a 1984-style omniscient state.

The battle is being waged on two fronts: one, domestic and public, is being fought by U.S. financial institutions and other groups through legal means. The individual battle is being fought by a growing throng of individuals and companies who are moving assets out of jurisdictions where privacy is under attack (e.g., the U.S.) to jurisdictions where privacy is revered and inviolable (e.g., Switzerland).

Why Use a Swiss Bank?

There are today three sound reasons why an investor should use a Swiss bank as a broker and custodian for his investments: safety, privacy and versatility.

Safety

Swiss banks have a record of safety unmatched by that of any other country. Accounts in Swiss banks are under close and strict control of Swiss regulatory authorities. Under the Federal Banking Act, all Swiss banks are subject to the supervision of the Federal Bank Commission in Bern, and also of the Swiss National Bank, to which they must submit their balance sheets at least twice a year. Each bank must maintain mandatory reserves and cash liquidity. Each bank is subject to both regular and unannounced audits by private accounting firms* certified by the banking authorities.

---

*Swiss bank secrecy laws apply to accounting firms in exactly the same manner as they do banks.

There is a further aspect to safety that applies particularly to investments in the precious metals. As economic conditions worsen, the danger arises of confiscation of both gold and silver held in commodity exchange inventories in the U.S., as happened in the economic turmoil of the 1930s.

At the end of 1933, with the market price of silver at about 44 cents an ounce — 75 percent above the depression low — unlimited Treasury purchases of newly mined silver at 64 cents an ounce were initiated under the authority of the Thomas Amendment and the Silver Purchase Act of 1934. The Secretary of the Treasury was directed to purchase silver at home and abroad until the market price reached the traditional mint price of $1.29 an ounce, or until the monetary value of the Treasury's silver stock reached one-third of the monetary value of its gold stock. Speculative buying was stimulated. Treasury and private speculative purchases quickly bid prices up to 80 cents, and large speculative profits were made. Then, as now, U.S. Treasury officials were chagrined that speculators were profiting from the (obvious) results of Treasury policies and felt that such greed should be punished. *The Treasury issued an edict that taxed domestic silver transactions 50 percent*, to "capture the windfall profits created by the Treasury."

The Treasury acquired altogether 3,200 million ounces of silver — nearly half of it in the four-year period 1934-37, and the remaining half in the subsequent two decades. *About 110 million ounces consisted of silver that was "nationalized" in mid-1934, when the administration required domestically held non-monetary silver to be turned in at 50 cents per fine ounce.* (The confiscatory 50 percent tax and actual physical confiscation of Commodity exchange stocks made it impossible for the New York Commodity Exchange to function, and silver trading had to be shut down completely.) Could this happen again to investors who hold silver in the U.S.? Perhaps it is unlikely, but there is this precedent.

Privacy

The U.S. brokerage industry today serves the regulatory whims of the SEC and the revenue demands of the IRS more effectively than it serves the investment interests of its clients.

In Switzerland, on the other hand, client privacy is of paramount importance.

Under Article 47 (1)(b) of the Swiss Federal Banking Act of 1934, it is prohibited — under penalty of imprisonment and fine — for any bank officer or employee to disclose any information with respect to a client's account to any individual or government official without the client's authorization. This invaluable Swiss secrecy is subject to only two exceptions: (a) upon the death of a client, his legal representative or successors are entitled to information about the account in order to make a lawful transfer of ownership; (b) in the event of a criminal prosecution, Swiss authorities are entitled only to such information about the account as is directly related to the alleged crime.

When you invest through a Swiss bank account you are legally liable for taxes your own government demands on your capital gains at the time you sell, just as you would be on any domestic investment. The only difference is that Swiss banks file no "information returns" with any government, and the taxpayer himself is obligated to report such transactions to his own government.

Switzerland imposes no taxes on profits earned on either bullion or coin transactions. Deposit account interest or dividends earned within Switzerland are taxed 35 percent. This tax is withheld by Swiss banks on all deposit accounts and remitted to the Swiss government with no disclosure of account holders' identities. Foreign depositors residing in countries having Double Taxation Treaties with Switzerland (e.g., the U.S. and Canada) can apply to the Swiss government and obtain a refund of a portion of the amount withheld and, of course, are then liable for their own domestic taxes. A depositor's application to the Swiss national government for a refund authorizes a notification being forwarded by them to the revenue bureau of the applicant's government; however, such an application can be deferred up to three years by citizens of the United States without loss of one's right to the refund.

Versatility

In the United States, the political monopoly-grant system has carved up the finance and investment industry into a series of narrow, licensed monopolies. Thus, the U.S. investor must enter into an insurance contract *only* with a licensed insurance company, he must deal *only* with a licensed real estate broker to purchase land, he must buy stocks or bonds *only* from a licensed stock and bond broker, he must purchase commodities *only* through a licensed commodity broker, he must deposit savings account or checking account funds *only* with a licensed bank, etc.

The Swiss financial and investment industry (banking) has not been artificially carved into many arbitrarily separate pieces. Swiss banks are multiple-purpose financial and investment service organizations. Swiss banks can and do perform all of the services performed by the half-dozen different U.S. financial institutions listed above.

Because they are so versatile, because they afford complete privacy, and because they have a long record of stability and safety — unmatched anywhere — Swiss banks attract the business of knowledgeable clients from all parts of the world, especially from countries which lack either the markets or the freedom for investors to employ their capital at home profitably and prudently.

One final reason to use a Swiss bank is to place some wealth abroad, before existing currency regulations on transfers out of the United States are tightened, and in case transfers are prohibited outright in a future emergency.

Beginning July 1, 1972, for example, under the *usurped* authority of Public Law 91-508 (never mind the Constitution regarding privacy of contracts), the United States Treasury removed the freedom legally to transfer abroad amounts of $5,000 or more in cash or "negotiable monetary instruments" *without reporting the details* of such transactions to the United States Treasury. (Transfers of funds by a bank check or cable need not be reported by the individual involved, but are, of course, a matter of record at the U.S. bank.)

These regulations *do not* prohibit such transfers. Strictly speaking, they are reporting requirements, not currency controls. However, it appears obvious that this is but a first legislative enabling step toward the imposition of outright currency controls in the future, perhaps soon, by administrative fiat.

Selecting a Swiss Bank

Swiss banks do not solicit clients for two reasons. First, they don't have to; their services are so much in demand that they can and do choose which client-applicants they will accept. Second, Switzerland is a very small country, and banking is already its largest industry; so Swiss banking regulations severely limit advertising and solicitation by banks — especially in countries where the privacy that Swiss banks afford may be opposed to official government policy.

Many Swiss banks do not handle silver bullion purchases. The "big five" Swiss banks will urge you to buy a "silver claim account." These accounts *do not* enable you to own actual bullion; they are merely bookkeeping entries whereby the bank undertakes to accept clients' money on the basis of the current silver price and to return the money at some future time based on the then-current price. Silver claim accounts are paper contracts only, as are futures contracts in New York or Chicago. They *are not recommended*, for the same reasons commodity futures contracts in the U.S. are not, i.e., because they are paper contracts only and there is some risk that, in the face of a sudden doubling or tripling of the silver price in a short time, and a severe physical shortage of silver (which I expect to recur in the future), a contracting bank or commodity exchange might be unable (or unwilling) to make delivery of bullion on demand. Some of the medium-sized and smaller Swiss banks will purchase, on clients' instructions, silver bullion and the other "hard money" investments recommended for cash (outright purchase) or on margin, with the bank loaning up to 50 percent of the total purchase amount.* This is

---

*The medium-sized, growing Swiss banks offer foreign clients the best combination of service and stability. Since early 1967, ERC has dealt with several banks in Zurich and Geneva. Through this experience ERC is in a position to recommend institutions that it has found to be exceptionally well managed.

The opening of a Swiss bank account and the transfer of funds can be facilitated through the use of simple procedures devised by the author. Information about these procedures can be obtained by writing to Economic Research Counselors, P.O. Box 91566, West Vancouver, British Columbia, Canada (offices at 212-585 16th Street) or by telephone: (604) 926-5476.

referred to as 2-to-1 leverage. Leverage enables the buyer to multiply his profits if the price moves up after the purchase. For example, on 50 percent margin, if the price rises 25 percent after the purchase, the capital gain is 50 percent (less fees and interest). And, it will multiply his losses if the price goes down from his purchase price.

The end of the inflationary road

CHAPTER TEN

Hyperinflation: The End — and the Beginning

In the ideological climate of today there can be no genuine reversal of monetary policy. The two-digit inflation must rage on,. . . The purchasing power of the dollar must fall at ever-faster rates, being depreciated by ever-larger injections of money and credit and a growing expectation thereof. Two-digit inflation only comes to an end with the advent of three-digit inflation which signals the approaching demise of the paper currency.
—Hans Sennholz
The Freeman Magazine

We are presently in the middle stages of a runaway inflation that began accelerating in the mid-1960s, which fed on itself in the 1970s and which is irreversible in the 1980s. Informed, intelligent observers should not be deceived by interludes of moderation in money and price inflation rates into believing that the long-run acceleration toward hyperinflation has been halted or reversed.

Many people talk of inflation *or* depression as if the two were alternate courses; as if there were a trade-off between them. To conquer depression (or recession) the Federal Reserve System in the United States or any other central bank will turn on the monetary machine and stimulate the economy at the cost of more inflation. This policy seems to work in the early stages of an inflation and did so until the 1970s. The trade-off exists only until an economy reaches the early runaway inflationary stage where it begins to feed on itself. Once this begins, inflation *plus* recession ensues, regardless of government policy. *And, with each successive bout, both effects become more extreme and more prolonged.* Here is the record for the last three recessions and what I consider to be a conservative projection:

	Consumer Prices	Wholesale Prices	Industrial Production	Duration
1960-61	+2.2%	+.2%	- 6%	9 months
1969-70	+5.6%	+2.6%	- 7%	12 months
1973-75	+15.8%	+24.4%	-13%	18 months
1980-82	+40.0% *	+60.0% *	-30% *	26 months*

*Projected minimums.

We have had three inflationary recessions already in the past two decades; we may well experience one or two more in the 1980s before the final hyperinflationary explosion. But the natural laws of cause-and-effect will eventually reign supreme, and "eventually" may be sooner than most of us would like to expect. The consequence will be rampant runaway inflation with the state unable to print paper dollars at a sufficient rate to compensate for explosively rising prices. In the final hyperinflationary collapse, daily and even hourly price surges may be seen as the money value of goods and services far outdistances printing-press increases in the paper money supply.

The Experience of Others

The world witnessed one such price explosion caused by hyperinflation in Germany following World War I. Just prior to the German crisis, politicians and government economists made loud claims that the economy was prospering. These claims were based on the fact that it took several years before the price level reached and surpassed the inflated money supply. The combined total of note circulations and bank deposits rose from 12 billion marks prior to World War I to 63 billion during the war, with prices lagging and only rising about 150 percent for the same time period. During these few years, it did indeed appear to the relatively uninformed public that the nation was prosperous. This relationship reversed itself in the years 1921 to the beginning of 1923, however, with the money supply merely doubling while prices quintupled. Throughout

Stupendous denominations on the currency were commonplace in Germany in 1923. The bills were printed on one side only because there was no time to let the ink dry. As hyperinflation accelerated through the year, billion-mark notes became common.

1922 and 1923, prices rose faster than the money supply. In August 1922, the country's money supply totalled 252 billion marks. In January 1923, it was 2 trillion. In September 1923, it stood at 28 quadrillion. And in November 1923, it reached 497 quintillion — that is, 497 followed by 18 zeros!

By mid-1923 Germans were paying a billion marks for a single loaf of bread! When prices began to soar at the rate of hourly increases and people realized the worthlessness of their currency, frustration, violence and chaos began erupting in major cities.

The same thing happened in a number of European and Asian countries following World War II — with the notable exception of Germany, which remembered the 1920s well. The case of Hungary was typical and the following first-hand account is instructive:

> What happens to a country when inflation goes completely wild? For a modern example, there's the experience of post-World War II Hungary, which in the summer of 1946 went through hyperinflation.

This room is papered with worthless German banknotes. In November 1923 when the mark had been hyperinflated to destruction, the new "rentenmark" was issued, each one was worth one trillion old marks.

"I remember one day eggs cost 1 million Hungarian pengos each. The next day, they jumped to 5 million pengos each," according to Ferenc Nagy, who had the unhappy distinction of being Prime Minister at that time. *And it moved from annual double-digit rates to daily double-digit rates in less than two years!* (Emphasis added.)

"In 1944, before the drastic inflation started, one U.S. dollar was worth 3½ pengos. By August 1946, one dollar was worth a trillion pengos.

"The price of a loaf of bread, which cost a third of a pengo in

1944, soared to a trillion pengos at the height of the inflation. Anyone with a small plot of ground on which he could grow food would find a line of people hopefully waiting to trade a pair of shoes or an old coat for something to eat."

Nagy, now in his 70s and living in Herndon, Va., further stated, in a newspaper interview: "We couldn't print new money fast enough. First the printers had to leave off the colored ink from the pengo bills, and then they had to stop putting serial numbers on them, the presses were working so fast.

"Our money had lost its value because when the Nazis left after occupying Hungary, they took all the gold reserves that had backed our currency. . .

"At the end of 1946 things got better. The U.S. Army had seized the gold in Berlin that the Nazis had stolen from our treasury, and returned it to us. With backing for our money, we abolished the discredited pengo and introduced a new unit of currency, the forint.

"The Hungarian people accepted it and were able to begin a program of reconstruction and recovery."*

The same nightmarish conditions can develop in present-day America. The present "balance" in the U.S. between the rates of price increase and money supply inflation is precarious at best, and it is only a matter of time before soaring prices out-distance increasing issues of fiat currency, as they did briefly in 1974 and again in most of 1979. During a renewed surge in double-digit price inflation the Washington gang will probably impose wage and price controls. This, along with disproportionate price increases of various raw commodities just before the imposition, will cause industrial manufacturers and farming producers to become still less willing or even able to risk the necessary capital to produce even essential goods. The resulting shortages, as always, will leave officials no choice but to lift the controls and will cause prices of virtually everything to skyrocket when they do.

This scenario will most likely be the prelude to the final hyperinflationary destruction of currencies.

*Quoted remarks from *The Enquirer.*

The Revolt Against Paper

The trigger for the final hyperinflationary explosion is a certain indefinable, critical level of public awareness and loss of (misplaced) confidence. Once that critical level of awareness is reached, the movement of the currency depreciation rate from double-digit percentages to triple-digits and then to total worthlessness can come in a few months, weeks, or even in only a matter of days.

> I think they will suddenly become aware of it, and the whole thing will be over within just a few days. It took the Germans 10 months to realize their paper money had no value after inflation started to run away. I think that because the U.S.A. is far more vulnerable than Germany, and we have much better financial communications than did the Germans in 1923, we will not even take 10 weeks, but more like 10 days. What I'm predicting is that once some big money lenders panic, it will not take more than 10 days for all the dominos to fall down instead of 10 months as in Germany. . . .
> Ten days later, the dollar will be worthless and moneylenders wiped out. A return to the gold standard and a balanced budget will be the only way to restore confidence.*

Furthermore, in the national hyperinflations of the past, sound foreign currencies were a financial haven for capital as the domestic currency became worthless. But "sound" has always meant redeemable in gold, and today no national currency is redeemable in gold. We are faced with a hyperinflation truly global in its proportions, the consequences of which will be far more devastating than those of past hyperinflations.

> The chaotic events of the German hyperinflation and other accelerated booms,. . .are only a pale shadow of what would happen under a World State inflation. For Germany was able to recover and return to a full monetary market economy quickly, since it could institute a new currency based on exchanges with other pre-existing moneys (foreign currencies). . .
> [But], no money can be established on the market except as it

*James Sibbet, editor of *Let's Talk Silver and Gold*. Sibbet Publications, Pasadena, California 91101.

can be exchanged for a previously-existing money (which in turn must have ultimately related back to a commodity in barter). *If a World State outlaws gold and silver and establishes a unitary fiat money, which it proceeds to inflate until a runaway boom destroys it, there will be no pre-existing money on the market.* The task of reconstruction will then be enormously more difficult.*

People rebel against a paper money that is in fact losing its purchasing value at a rapid rate for the same reason they rebel against confiscatory taxes — they cannot afford not to.

Once this phase begins, it proceeds like a whirlwind and in a very short time the currency is worthless. Once this phase begins, it is too late to take defensive measures to protect one's savings from destruction. All the elements for this to begin anytime were in place in the late 1970s — I think the hyper-inflationary blow-up will occur sometime in the 1980s. Every informed person should take defensive action immediately, well ahead of the obvious beginning of hyperinflation.

That is why I am sticking my neck out *now*, ahead of the ob-vious beginning, even though I may be way off on how soon inflation will actually reach this terminal hyperinflationary stage. If I waited until I was sure of the timing, the informa-tion would be too late to help you.

Danger and Opportunity

This is *not* a pessimistic outlook for the American people, or for any other peoples. The great damage — ravaging people around the world — occurs *during* the course of rampant statism and runaway inflation. When hyperinflation takes over, it means that people are spontaneously throwing off the monetary yoke of systematic looting with which their respec-tive nation-state hierarchies have bled away their substance for generations. It means danger but it also means opportuni-ty.

At that critical juncture, which means the total destruction

*Murray N. Rothbard, *Man, Economy and State* (Los Angeles: Nash Publishing Company, 1962), p. 877.

of nation-state paper currencies, the way will be prepared economically for a new and unprecedented era of prosperity and progress — *provided* that there exists enough economic understanding among the ideological opinion molders in society for markets to be left politically free to provide sound money competitively along with various other market services.

Indeed, herein lies the reason for long-term optimism. For this emerging depression can be best understood as the triumph of the orderly, harmonious, natural laws of human behavior and economics, over the disorderly, coercive, capricious "laws" of the state. It has been so with all runaway inflations throughout history, although, in the past, few of the participants had much comprehension of the laws which govern human action.

In the present inflation, however, for the first time in history, there is comparatively widespread and growing economic understanding of appropriate solutions, especially in the vital field of monetary economics. Much of the requisite understanding is contained in that body of economic knowledge called the "Austrian School." No other economic theorists are able to apply their theories so completely to practical life.

The Austrian School economists (most notably Karl Menger, Eugen von Böhm-Bawerk, Ludwig von Mises, Friedrich Hayek, Murray Rothbard and Hans Sennholz — with only the latter three living), were the first to apply *a priori* reasoning (deduced from self-evident propositions) to the study of human action in general and economics in particular. This approach is in contrast to the *a posteriori* method (induced from observed historical information).* It has enabled the Austrians intellectually to construct and study the free-market economy — even though one has never existed. These methods have further enabled them to compare the workings of this abstract,

---

*This distinction is characteristic of these two different approaches to economics; however, most economists, including me, make use of both reasoning methods, depending upon their judgment of which is more appropriate to the subject matter and purpose of a particular analysis. And, of course, it is always appropriate to check one's conclusions against the observable facts available.

conceived free-market economy with the workings of the concrete, perceived, heavily regulated economy.

The Austrian economists do not presently influence the President, other officials, or Congress. However, their theories and analyses have influenced a large and growing number of private individuals, particularly during the past decade. These individuals' increased understanding of the economic situation has proven immensely profitable for some of them as investors in recent times, while the past decade has not treated kindly others who have ignored the Austrian analysis. This understanding can be expected to spread and to broaden its impact in the future, and eventually to have a dramatic and beneficial effect on overall economic and social well-being.

The Nature and Source of the Problem

We are subjective inhabitants of an objective universe. We do *not* each perceive and interpret the world around us in the same way. Therefore, we do not each act and react to the physical world, nor interact with others, in the same way. Yet, we *do* share the same reality — both as to the physical world *and* as to each other.

If we act in an unrealistic manner in the physical world, we soon learn to act differently — "the burnt child fears the fire." However, an unrealistic action in the social sphere, affecting others, may not have an immediate "burnt finger" impact on the actor. Somebody else's finger is burned. Similarly, of course, we are each adversely affected by the wrong actions of others. But, in social actions, cause and effect are separated as to person, and often as to time and space, and the true and full consequences of a given unrealistic and destructive action are more obscure. Learning is more difficult.

The problem is compounded, if, over a period, destructive action gains the sanction of convention and peer approval (e.g., cannibalism in some tribal societies) because such sanction and approval tends to substitute for individual inquiry and thought in the adoption of standards for decisions and choices in social action. The problem is further compounded if such destructive actions become institutionalized and propagated by an organization (e.g., human sacrifice by a group of religious fanatics) because the destructive action, supported by an ideology and a set of superstitions, acquires an aura of positive virtue to the organization's members. And, individual thought about the advisability of such actions is virtually eliminated.

The problem is still further and greatly compounded when whole codified patterns of such destructive actions gain sanction, approval, a supportive ideology backed by superstitions and an aura of virtue, *and are enforced* by an organization which has a monopoly on the use of force.

That organization is the state. Its ideology is statism, its principal superstitions are that state coercion and plunder are positive, productive and virtuous actions.

The greatest problem facing the world today is rampant statism.

Statism vs. Economics

Modern totalitarian statism is the overriding social issue of all time — an issue that overshadows all markets and affects all investments. It is the underlying but seldom-discussed cause of all major social crises.

In its extreme totalitarian form — toward which we are headed — statism is not merely a bothersome bureaucracy. The trend throughout this century, so far, is unmistakable and statism's appetite is insatiable.

> Totalitarianism is much more than mere bureaucracy. It is the subordination of every individual's whole life, work, and leisure, to the orders of those in power and office. It is the reduction of man to a cog in an all-embracing machine of compulsion and coercion. It forces the individual to renounce any activity of which the government does not approve. It tolerates no expression of dissent. It is the transformation of society into a strictly disciplined labor-army (as the advocates of socialism say) or into a penitentiary (as the opponents say). At any rate it is the radical break from the way of life to which the civilized nations clung in the past. . .

> [Modern socialism] is totalitarian in the strict sense of the term. It holds the individual in tight rein from the womb to the tomb. At every instant of his life the "comrade" is bound to obey implicitly the orders issued by the supreme authority. The State is both his guardian and his employer. The State determines his work, his diet, and his pleasures. The State tells him what to think and what to believe in.*

Either there will emerge a fundamental change in our conceptions and actions concerning "government" within this decade, or we will have all our investments confiscated and become either employees or prisoners of the state.

Economics is the study of *voluntary human action*, choice and behavior and, therefore, necessarily of life. *Life*, intelligent, *valuing* life, is a prerequisite to choice and action and therefore to the subject matter of economics. Economics is the study of voluntary human actions aimed at increasing life's satisfactions and decreasing life's dissatisfactions, and of the *appropriate means* by which these life improvements can be most effectively achieved. Well understood, the great economic truth is that what is an *appropriate means* (voluntary, peaceful means) is the same for all individuals whether their interests are viewed singly or collectively.

The People vs. the State

The totalitarian state, by its nature, structure and methods, is an appropriate mechanism for only two purposes: plunder and destruction. In so-called peacetime, the principal activity of such a state is to hinder and plunder the productive inhabitants of its territory for the benefit of its unproductive, plundering supporters. As the desire for plunder is insatiable, there is no inherent limit to the growth of the state mechanism. However, there is an extraneous limit — the maximum plunder rate that the productive inhabitants can endure and/or are willing to sanction and tolerate.

States inevitably tend periodically to bump up against this upper limit and try to exceed it. This attempt repeatedly produces a depression which reduces the proportionate size of the

*Ludwig von Mises in *Bureaucracy*.

state (relative to total production) again to an endurable and tolerable level (resulting in what is erroneously called "the business cycle" or "trade cycle"). Under the conditions of a rapid growth of excessive state coercion and plunder and/or a great reduction in the level of the population's sanction and toleration of coercion and plunder, the result is a revolution which sharply reduces the size, scope and power of the residual or succeeding state mechanism. Under these conditions, a sufficiently widespread withdrawal of sanction and lowering of toleration can result in the elimination of the totalitarian state.

As remote as this may seem, it is the only possible solution to the increasingly urgent problem of the rampant growth of these malignant monsters.

Any efforts to reform the state are worse than futile as their only possible outcome would be to delay the day of reckoning for statism. The energies and intelligence of such efforts will be much more positively and fruitfully employed if directed at lowering the victim populations' tolerance of coercion and plunder.*

Ideology and Freedom

Ideas precede action, not just for individuals but for societies too. The past decade has witnessed increasing public disenchantment with the state and its deeds. At the same time, public interest in free-market alternatives has increased markedly. This improvement is well illustrated by the contrast

*"All of this havoc, this misfortune, this ruin, descends upon you not from alien foes, but from the one enemy whom you yourselves render as powerful as he is, for whom you bravely go to war, for whose greatness you do not refuse to offer your own bodies unto death. He who thus domineers over you has only two eyes, only two hands, only one body, no more than is possessed by the least man among the (multitudinous) numbers dwelling in your cities; he has indeed nothing more than the power that you confer upon him to destroy you. . .*Resolve to serve no more, and you are at once freed.*" (Emphasis added.)
— Etienne de la Boetie in A *Discourse on Voluntary Servitude.*

between the pessimism contained in *apropos* remarks made by Friedrich Hayek (in 1967) and the optimism expressed by Murray N. Rothbard (in 1973).

Pessimistic (1967):

We must make the building of a free society once more an intellectual adventure, a deed of courage. What we lack is a liberal Utopia, a programme which seems neither a mere defence of things as they are nor a diluted kind of socialism, but a truly liberal radicalism. . .which does not confine itself to what appears today as politically possible. We need intellectual leaders who are prepared to resist the blandishments of power and influence and who are willing to work for an ideal, however small may be the prospects of its early realization. They must be men who are willing to stick to principles and to fight for their full realization, however remote. . . . Free trade and freedom of opportunity are ideals which still may rouse the imaginations of large numbers, but a mere "reasonable freedom of trade" or a mere "relaxation of controls" is neither intellectually respectable nor likely to inspire any enthusiasm. The main lesson which the true liberal must learn from the success of the socialists is that it was their courage to be Utopian which gained them the support of the intellectuals and thereby an influence on public opinion. . . . Unless we can make the philosophic foundations of a free society once more a living intellectual issue, and its implementation a task which challenges the ingenuity and imagination of our liveliest minds, the prospects of freedom are indeed dark. But if we can regain that belief in the power of ideas which was the mark of liberalism at its best, the battle is not lost.*

Optimistic (1973):

The libertarian creed. . .offers the fulfillment of the best of the American past along with the promise of a far better future. Even more than conservatives, who are often attached to the monarchical traditions of a happily obsolete European past, libertarians are squarely in the great classical liberal tradition that built the United States and bestowed on us the American heritage of individual liberty, a peaceful foreign

*Friedrich Hayek, "The Intellectuals and Socialism," *Studies in Philosophy, Politics and Economics* (Chicago: University of Chicago Press, 1967), p. 194.

policy, minimal government, a free-market economy. Libertarians are the only genuine current heirs of Jefferson, Paine, Jackson and the abolitionists. . . .

Strands and remnants of libertarian doctrines are, indeed, all around us, in large parts of our glorious past and in values and ideas in the confused present. But only libertarianism takes these strands and remnants and integrates them into a mighty, logical, and consistent system. The enormous success of Karl Marx and Marxism has been due not to the validity of his ideas — all of which, indeed, are fallacious — but to the fact that he dared to weave socialist theory into a mighty system. Liberty cannot succeed without an equivalent and contrasting systematic theory; and until the last few years, despite our great heritage of economic and political thought and practice, we have not had a fully integrated and consistent theory of liberty. We now have that systematic theory; we come, fully armed with our knowledge, prepared to bring our message and to capture the imagination of all groups and strands in the population. All other theories and systems have clearly failed: socialism is in retreat everywhere, and notably in Eastern Europe; liberalism has bogged us down in a host of insoluble problems; conservatism has nothing to offer but sterile defense of the *status quo*. Liberty has never been fully tried in the modern world; libertarians now propose to fulfill the American dream and the world dream of liberty and prosperity for all mankind.*

We are rapidly approaching a time when the dollar will be rendered worthless, when the precious metals will again become recognized as money; indeed, when free competitive markets may well foster even *better* money and money systems. For those able to protect their assets and themselves, there are manifold opportunities to disseminate the ideas which can slowly move society in a new direction — away from statism and stagnation and toward freedom and prosperity.

*Murray N. Rothbard, *For a New Liberty*, revised ed. (New York: Collier 1978) p.321.

MONEY   STATE

CHAPTER ELEVEN

The Separation of Money and State

. . . ideas that are really sound . . . grow stronger, as the social
system to which they are opposed becomes more and more obsolete.

—W.E. Woodward
A New American History

Greater than the tread of mighty armies is an idea whose time
has come.

—Victor Hugo
History of a Crime

We live in a world of constantly rising prices. Not only are
prices generally rising; they are generally rising in terms of all
currencies — including even the Swiss franc. The only distinction between one currency and another today in this respect is
the rapidity and extent of the relative price rises. It is, of
course, quite normal for prices to fluctuate, with some going
up and some going down, to reflect changing patterns of supply and demand for various goods in the market. However,
when prices overall — the general price level — move up and
up and up over a period of time, there is only one explanation:
the price mechanism is not reflecting normal market factors. It
is, rather, reflecting inflationary increases in the supply of
money units and the consequent depreciation in the purchasing value of the units.

Hence we are seeing the results of a perverse competition
being conducted by the political managers of national currencies. We are seeing the results today of the decades-long
salami-slicing abandonment by national governments of virtually all of the tried and proven principles that are requisite
to sound circulating money and to a smoothly functioning

139

payments system. We are witnessing the vain attempts of central bankers to "manage" their currencies without benefit of any of the self-correcting mechanisms of the more-or-less sound money systems of the past.

The very existence of political "management" of money is a grotesque and destructive distortion of sound money principles. The only rule needed to aid the existence and smooth functioning of money is the (commercially developed) merchant-law and common-law proscription against fraud. Sound money depends on free markets and the *absence* of any arbitrary authority over either the unit or the system itself.

Under an international gold standard system, such as existed in the century preceding the World War I era, nearly all aspects of international and domestic monetary systems are self-correcting. The general price level in any given place remains fairly uniform over time under such a system, simply because the supply of money units in the system is virtually fixed over any given time period. Prices may even decline somewhat, reflecting technological improvements in productivity and in the overall level and availability of goods and services in the market. Redeemability of currencies for gold (and/or silver) and the consequent physical movements of precious metals in settlement of balances serve both as a barometer of the integrity of any particular currency and as a certain check-rein on any excessive issues of currencies.

The merits of the gold standard system, limiting the extent and duration of irresponsible official action in monetary matters, caused officials to seek the mitigation of these limitations during and after World War I. With the formalization of the "gold-exchange" standard system in 1922 the U.S. dollar and the pound sterling were in effect elevated to an equivalent status with gold itself in international payments and, ostensibly, as reserve backing in the central bank coffers of other nations for issues of their own currencies. Thus "paper gold" was invented in the 1920s and the political procedures were put in place that facilitated the following six decades of national *and* international official counterfeiting of paper money and destruction of its value.

Just briefly, some of the consequences directly traceable to that monumental arrogation of arbitrary power are the capital markets inflation of the 1920s, the crash, depression and trade war of the 1930s (as an indirect consequence, at least), the shooting war of the 1940s, the post-World War II economic and monetary chaos in Europe and in Asia, and the three decades of accelerating global inflation and its accompanying distortions since World War II.

Thus, through perseverance on the part of national monetary officials in fixing things that aren't broken and through their persistence in adopting policies and procedures that will have the opposite effect to that which is announced, we now find ourselves in that paper money enthusiasts' heaven where all stops of every sort to further accelerating inflation have been totally removed. We have that blissful state of a global network, a rather shattered one, of 100 percent fiat currencies backed by nothing whatsoever, not the shadow of a promise nor even the slightest hope of any future redemption at anything more than a tiny, tiny fraction of current values.

An Equitable System

The world sorely needs an equitable and smoothly functioning money unit and money system. In the absence of banking laws that exempt bankers from the common-law responsibilities of warehousemen, and in the absence of state monopolies on currency issue, such a unit and such a system would evolve naturally in the market. In fact, such a system has existed in the past, and would re-emerge and be improved upon if bankers and states were to lose their criminal and anti-competitive legal monopolies.

The money units in the various nation-states, and the world monetary network that exists today, have devolved from the the gold-standard system that evolved spontaneously from the barter system more than 3,000 years ago. Variations of the gold standard have existed in various parts of the world throughout recorded history and have functioned more or less well in proportion to how little or how much the local ruler interfered.

The use of a gold standard does not completely preclude inflation, as some people believe, but as long as the rules are observed it does limit inflationary possibilities and it does preclude anyone gaining an unearned benefit or suffering an inequity from inflation. The problem, of course, is getting governments to abide by the rules.

The history of state involvement with money is a history of destructive involvement, even though the original express purpose was for the state to administer the system for the benefit of all, to put its certification on the coins and later the notes, to assure everyone in the market that the money is genuine. But in practice the opposite has always resulted. In every instance where money has circulated without government interference, competition has kept it honest. In every instance throughout history when governments have become involved, money has become dishonest and in most instances it has eventually been hyperinflated to destruction.

The problem occurs because it is the nature of the officials of states to recognize no limits to their power other than those that are eventually forced upon them by reality. It takes a long time to destroy a sound money system; it has taken nearly a century to destroy the present one.

If today's system had been installed a century ago, it would have collapsed in a matter of a few months. But this process has taken many decades wherein, bit by bit, first one safeguard then another has been removed, in a long series of often minuscule steps bringing us from fully redeemable genuine paper money to completely irredeemable fiat paper money.

Understanding the Political Beast

Many people are convinced that we have got to do something in the political arena to solve the money problem. Various efforts are made in congressional lobbying, and in proselytizing the public, in an effort to bring back the gold standard, to make the dollar again as "good as gold." This has no possibility of success in my opinion. The solution to today's money problem doesn't rest in the supply side of the ideological market in politics. There is an infinite potential supply of political interventions into the market. We need to work on the demand side of the ideological market equation.

As long as there is a demand for increasing government services, handouts and favors, no politician or official is going to refuse to meet that demand and cause himself not to be reelected or reappointed. It is a total waste of time — worse, it is damaging, in my opinion — to work with or try to "influence" bureaucrats, legislators, officials and politicians. They are generally acting in accordance with their essentially predatory natures and, as a body, will always do so.

Why do I call them predators? I'm trying to help you to understand the problem, or at least to understand it in a way that I think it should be understood. These people hold an underlying belief that justifies what they do. And essentially that underlying belief is: they can manage your life better than you can. And this end justifies the means, in their minds. It gives them, in their own thinking, a justification for what they do. A penetrating observation by G.K. Chesterton highlights the nature of this problem:

> Despotism and attempts at despotism are a disease. They are a disease of the spirit. They represent as it were the drunkenness of power. It is when men in power begin to grow desperate, when they are overwhelmed with the difficulties and blunders of humanity, that they fall back upon the wild desire to manage everything themselves. This belief that all would go right if we could only get the strings into our own hands, is a fallacy, almost without exception. But nobody can say it is not public spirited. The sin and the sorrow of despotism is not that it does not love men but it loves them too much and trusts them too little.

I would add that it loves power too much and trusts markets too little. Politicians and officials don't understand the economics of free markets, they don't know there are countervailing forces that prevent monopolies from having long-term success, that competition doesn't need to be regulated — that it needs to be let alone in the context of the free market to be effective. And yet they sincerely believe that they can regulate these matters and everything else in your life for your greater benefit. For this reason, they consider their own reelection or reappointment — at any cost — to be of paramount importance.

Enthroning Ignorance

Government should not be doing the things that it does because of the nature of legislators. The following quote from Orin Hatch of Utah illustrates Congress's incompetence in passing regulatory legislation:

> Did we realize the cost of these regulations in terms of lost productivity when we passed them? Who would admit that we knew this and consciously took action to reduce the living standards of the American people and the job opportunities of our children? On the other hand, if we deny that we knew, it amounts to an admission that we legislate without knowing what we are doing. Which admission do we prefer — that we consciously harm the people or that we don't know what we are doing?

I don't think that they consciously intend to harm the people but they don't know very much about what they are doing to you and they certainly don't know it as well as you. The only sensible thing that a thoughtful person can say to any legislator is: "Do nothing and you'll be doing the best you are capable of doing."

Subsidizing Interference

Government should not be doing the things that it does because of the nature of bureaucrats and bureaucracy. Bureaucrats succeed within the structure of bureaucracy by not making waves — they delay things, they avoid decisions and yet they demand to be consulted on all aspects of business enterprise.

Dr. Carl Zimmerer, managing director of *Interfinanz*, a West German firm specializing in arranging mergers and acquisitions, said in a recent annual report:

> The number of government agencies which have to be approached before a transaction is completed is growing. . .If the

numerous new civil servants would merely take their pay-checks and do nothing in return, this would only be objection-able from the taxpayer's point of view; but some of these officials actually insist on working, and that is what makes the swollen bureaucracy such a burden for industry. They all want to be consulted, but none of them want to make a decision. Higher salaries and promotion do not go to the official who was successful in producing results in the national interest, but to the one who had no bad experience. And the ones who, in the interests of the industrial sector, give their rapid consent to requests, do occasionally go wrong and get condemned.

Bureaucrats are incapable of making decisions without spreading responsibility, which means they've got to get 16 other bureaucrats to agree with them before anything hap-pens, and the delay and the cost are enormous. Earlier this year, for example, the Small Business Administration reported that government paper work costs small businesses $12.7 billion a year!

How can even the most rabid supporter of state interference in markets proclaim its effectiveness in the face of such enor-mous costs and such negative results?

Corruption Masked as Government

Government should not be doing the things that it does because of the corrupt nature of political administration. All political administration is corrupt in a system wherein favors from "the public treasury" are coin for reelection or reappoint-ment. To highlight this I quote a penetrating analysis made several years ago by a former Mayor of Cleveland, Mr. Tom Johnson, in addressing the question of the nature of corruption in a discussion with a reporter — he was condemning the reporter's lack of political understanding:

> First you thought it was bad politicians, then you found out that many of them were well intentioned, then you blamed the bad businessmen who bribed these well intentioned poli-ticians. Then you discovered that not all businessmen bribe politicians, and many of those who did were pretty good businessmen. So you found out that mostly it was big business-men that bribed politicians and that little businessmen didn't so you invented the term "big business" and that is as far as

your analysis went. Hell, can't you see that it is privileged business that corrupts politics — whether it is a big steam railroad that wants a franchise or a little gambling house that wants not to be raided, a temperance society that wants a law passed, a poor little prostitute that wants to be let alone or a merchant occupying storage space in an alley — it's those who seek and/or possess privilege who corrupt. It's those who possess privilege that defend our current system — can't you see that?

More recently, a front page news item summary from *Barron's* (January 21, 1980) highlighted a network of corruption on the national level:

> From Maine to Texas, a crescent of corruption. Recent conviction of Anthony Scotto, ILA organizer, for taking payoffs is merely tip of iceberg. Far-flung FBI probe of union racketeering leads to indictments, trials on Atlantic, Gulf coasts. *Widespread political links.* [Emphasis added.]

The Short-Sighted Electorate

Finally, government should not be doing the things it does because of the nature of the electorate majority. People vote ignorantly, and most often wrongly, because they lack knowledge of what would be the best solution even conceding that the issue at hand fairly states a genuine problem (which it often does not). They just don't know enough about most issues to vote intelligently. Instead, they vote in their superficially perceived self-interest. For anybody who is on the welfare rolls, for example, it is obviously to their advantage to vote for more welfare and for the politician who is promising more. But it is against the welfare of taxpayers generally to pay for special interest groups' favors. And, in the long run, it is against these same voters' personal self-interest if they really understood things.

This is the way in which congressmen and other elected officials get reelected. The nature of the political process is such that the public generally perceives that there is something wrong in the political arena and wants to see it redressed. . . politically! A poll of 1600 adults reported by AP in March 1979 found that only one person in five rated Congress as doing a good or excellent job but, by contrast, one in two thought that the Congressman in their own district was doing a good job.

This is a consequence of dividing responsibility to the point where there is no responsibility. And in the democratic political process, it works. Congress can do a horrible job and can be disapproved of by 4 out of 5 people — and yet, each Congressman running in his local district has better than a 50-50 chance of getting reelected.

The democratic process rests on the assumption that a majority is well-informed and deliberative on any subject. The fact is, however, that at any given time there are hundreds of proposals that are subjects of the democratic process, either in the voting of legislators or at election time amongst the population in general — and no one person casting a vote in the Congress or a ballot in an election could possibly be well-informed on the hundreds of issues involved. If you average out ignorance, you get an ignorant result — and that is what we have got.

With the principles of the original American republic largely forgotten (actually, never learned by most people alive today), with statist zealots in charge of the destructive mechanisms of "government," and with most businessmen and consumers alike looking to the state for favors and handouts, the ignorant result is that the American nation today is in fact, though not in name, a national-socialist state.

The Reinstitution of Honest Money

The fundamental solution to the problem with money is the separation of money and state. There is no possibility of a solution within state mechanisms. While I am certainly sympathetic with those people who are trying to limit government deficits with the idea of restoring some semblance of stability to the value of the national currencies, I believe that the ultimate solution is completely outside the state mechanism. I believe that the separation of money and state will produce more material and intangible good for people generally than the large amount of good that was accomplished by the separation of church and state.

The end result of the road we are travelling will be the destruction of national currencies and, with that, one of two outcomes. Either the nation-states will return to currencies fully redeemable in gold or silver (in the present context it would most likely be gold) or entrepreneurs in the markets will be given the opportunity by official default (by procrastination on the part of governments to agree officially on what to do) to innovate and establish a sound and enduring money. It is possible that there may be a hiatus between the destruction of the national currencies and the institution of a sound replacement money, a period, somewhat chaotic perhaps, in which there will be no media of exchange internationally and only those alternative media of exchange in domestic transactions that people adopt on their own initiative, such as silver coins for small transactions, and gold coins for larger transactions.

But that period will be fertile ground for the emergence of an entirely new and far better market-initiated and market-instituted money. Private entrepreneurs in free markets are deservedly famous for providing products and services that are of value and demanded by markets. Certainly the markets today are crying out for sound money. Further, as the following remarks demonstrate, I am joined in my conviction that only through free markets can we achieve a sound money by one of the most respected economists alive today.

> . . . There is no hope of ever again having decent money, unless we take from government the monopoly of issuing money . . . I am more convinced than ever that if we ever again are going to have a decent money, it will not come from government: it will be issued by private enterprise, because providing the public with good money which it can trust and use can not only be an extremely profitable business, it imposes on the issuer a discipline to which the government has never been and cannot be subject. It is a business which competing enterprise can maintain only if it gives the public as good a money as anybody else. . . .
>
> I am convinced that the hope of ever again placing on government this discipline is gone. . . .
>
> My conviction is that the hope of returning to the kind of gold standard system which has worked fairly well over a long

period is absolutely vain. Even if, by some international trea-
ty, the gold standard were reintroduced, there is not the
slightest hope that governments will play the game according
to the rules. . . We must hope that some of the more enter-
prising and intelligent financiers will soon begin to experiment
with [issuing a private money]. The great obstacle is that it involves such great changes in the whole financial structure that,
and I am saying this from the experience of many discussions,
no senior banker, who understands only the present banking
system, can really conceive how such a new system would
work, and he would not dare to risk and experiment with it. I
think we will have to count on a few younger and more flexible
brains to begin and show that such a thing can be done.*

Given that physical assets — the real capital — are not
destroyed by hyperinflation (only dollar-denominated paper
assets are actually destroyed), and given that very large and
diverse pools of capital are managed by institutional fund
managers (such as the insurance industry, pension funds,
mutual funds, etc.), and given the development of modern
markets for equities (in both producing companies and raw
commodities) there is technically and practically no reason
why we couldn't have a money that represented productive,
employed capital generally. And this could be done in the
same fashion that mutual funds operate but on a broader,
more diversified scale and a more refined basis of operation.
Such a money would represent the marriage of interest earnings and what are commonly called profits. In the long run
they are both derived from the earnings of capital, and those
who are risk takers will take the profits while those who want
a certain return will receive interest.

With a broad enough base, widely diversified in virtually all
forms of capital, a global mutual fund or unit trust, whose
share ownership was also globally dispersed, could form the
basis for a new, modern, sound money superior to any that has
ever existed — money that would appreciate quite consistently
over any period of a few years or more.

To solve the money problem we only require government to

*F.A. Hayek, 1974 Noble Laureate, from a lecture delivered at the Gold and
Monetary Conference, New Orleans, La., November 10, 1977.

stand aside and permit private companies to issue money. And probably a wide variety of things would be attempted, most of them probably failing. But market processes being what they are, and the need for sound money being so great, it would only be a short period of time before the markets would sort out who had the best product and was administering it in the most satisfactory way.

It is not the function of government to issue money and it should be crystal clear by now that state officials have completely discredited themselves in such a role. It is high time for markets to abandon the official scrip and to furnish their own sound media of exchange — money of genuine and increasing value, administered with integrity.*

---

*For a fuller explanation of the rationale and practicality of entrepreneurially issued, competitively marketed, capital-based money see *The Reinstitution of Money* (ERC Publishing Company, 212-585 16th Street, West Vancouver, British Columbia, Canada).

Epilogue

All men recognize the right of revolution; that is, the right to
refuse allegiance to and to resist the government, when its tyranny or its inefficiency are great and unendurable.
— Henry David Thoreau

Modern totalitarian states have enslaved virtually the entire
populations of their respective territories through generations of
indoctrination in state schools, propaganda in the popular press
and, in recent decades, via the regulated and coerced radio and
television media. There is little hope in sight for the brainwashed
adult majority. There is a very positive prospect, however, for a
more thoughtful minority who, with an enlightened perception
of their true power, can change the world and bring forth a
rebirth of the true liberalism of the American revolution — "with
liberty and justice for all."

It is always a minority that changes the course of a civilization. Their potential to effect change increases in proportion to
the degree the leaders of the majority are out of tune with the
best interests of the majority as circulated among opinion
molders. Their potential also increases in proportion to the
quality and consistency of their literature. The "peaceful revolution" has already begun on this fundamental level.

It is becoming increasingly clear to a growing segment of the
opinion molders, in and out of the media, that a totally controlled economy (communism) is a permanently depressed one
and that an interventionist economy, while regularly repressed,
is periodically depressed — with great damage to the interests of
the majority in both cases. Simultaneously, based on the work of
the late Ludwig von Mises, there is a growing body of literature
emanating from the Austrian School economists of today, most
notably Dr. Murray N. Rothbard, that is of exceptional quality
and which is consistently free market, pro-individual rights and

151

anti-interventionist — and consistently in the true best interests of the majority.

This revolution is aimed at nothing short of the complete dismantling of *all* government regulation of the economy and of all government involvement in the economy that is not strictly and directly related to bare bones government functions, based on the narrowest possible definitions. Of paramount importance to the success of this revolution is the separation of money and state, i.e., the repeal of the Federal Reserve Act and the legal tender laws. This immediately accomplishes two vital objectives. First, it facilitates the re-emergence of sound, competitive money in the markets. And second, it removes the source of state financing for wars and other grandiose but unpopular expenditures.

Next in urgency is the elimination of all regulatory bureaus of every description. Beyond merely restoring government to the limited functions and dimensions approved by the founders of the American republic, this revolution aims at whittling it down still more. It aims at the liquidation of the present American superstate, at the bankruptcy auction of all of its considerable real estate and other assets superfluous to narrowly defined government functions, and, thereby, at the retirement of its existing debts on however many cents-to-the-dollar that such liquidation would bring. In short, it aims at Thoreau's ideal of "a government that governs not at all."

No one need be concerned about how far down this road we can travel. Great accomplishments require great goals. We are aiming at perfection knowing full well that it is beyond human attainment — but also knowing full well that every step in the direction of that goal will enhance human liberty, progress, prosperity, peace and happiness.

If you can't join them, beat them.

Join the new American revolution!

Appendices

APPENDIX I

The Track Record Thus Far

—Christopher P. Weber
Editor-in-Chief
World Market Perspective

The overall objective of the ERC companies is the identification and application of economic ideas having long-term significance.

The first of the ERC group of companies, Economic Research Counselors, was founded in January 1967 by Jerome F. Smith. Mr. Smith also founded Economic Research Corporation as a separate research company in 1968 (succeeded by Economic Research Council establishment in 1974) and ERC Publishing Company in 1974.

Economic Research Council specializes in research and identification, ERC Publishing Company specializes in analysis and interpretation and Economic Research Counselors specializes in application and counseling. Each of these ERC firms is fundamentally different in theory and practice from the usual advisory service or brokerage house. Unlike most other advisors, ERC does not make numerous nor frequent recommendations, nor undertake to provide all-inclusive financial advice on one's total investment program. ERC research is focused at any one time on only a few recommendations — those few that our studies show have the highest long-term profit potential and a limited risk, based upon a careful analysis and interpretation of fundamental economic factors and application to the needs of individual clients.

ERC Publishing Company (212-585 16th Street, West Vancouver, B.C., Canada V7V 4S2) presents its recommendations to clients and selected prospective clients through comprehensive publications. Detailed explanation and discussion of new recommendations, and updated information on all current ones, is regularly published in the monthly economic newsletter, *World Market Perspective*, edited and produced under the direction of Mr. Smith.

Economic Research Counselors (also at 212-585 16th Street, West Vancouver, B.C., Canada V7V 4S2) provides personal assistance to clients. Basic research conclusions and recommendations may be useless without appropriate means to implement them; therefore before ERC makes any recommendations, its staff develop carefully selected trading and banking channels which are recommended for clients' use in implementing these recommendations.

Since January 1967, when ERC concluded that the U.S. Treasury's fixed redemption prices for silver and gold would have to be abandoned and that the dollar prices for gold and silver would begin a long and significant rise, the ERC Group companies have recommended gold and silver. Silver, then available at the suppressed price of $1.30 per ounce, was first to soar in price, beginning in May 1967, and was a precursor to gold, which did so nine months later.* From 1970 until October, 1978, we also recommended Swiss franc deposits, and platinum was recommended in August, 1977, when we concluded it was heavily under-valued in relation to the other precious metals.

The First Signal: The following table sets out the performance of various investments over the period beginning immediately after the official March, 1968, milestone announcement that

---

*It was not legal for U.S. residents to own gold bullion until the end of 1974. The first ERC gold recommendation was published in late 1971 — just shortly before gold began its rapid advance. The recommendation was to buy Old British Sovereign gold coins, which were legal to own. Priced in 1971 at $13.00 each, they are now (April 3, 1980) $143.00 or 1000 percent higher.

The first ERC recommendation to buy silver bullion was made in January, 1967, just four months before silver's historic rise began. The price then was $1.30. The gain to date is 1035 percent.

official monetary gold would no longer be available to markets at or near the officially supported price of $35 an ounce.

TABLE I

	Gold	Silver	Swiss Franc*	D.J.I.A.**	$Dep.a/c at 6%***
Mar. 16, 1968	$ 39.00	$ 2.49	.2295	830.90	$1,000.
Mar. 21, 1980	$525.00	$21.01	.5634	785.15	$2,035.
Change	+1246%	+743%	+145%	-5%	+104%

*Ignores interest earnings. **Ignores dividend yield. ***Pre-tax.

The Second Signal that a period of runaway inflation was ahead and would not be officially countered came August 15, 1971, when, on the heels of a second-quarter record U.S. balance-of-payments deficit and consequent flight from the dollar, Richard Nixon announced that the U.S. would "temporarily" suspend the international convertibility of the dollar into gold at $35. We predicted then that the dollar would be devalued by year-end 1971 (which it was), and urged further purchases of silver, gold and Swiss francs.

Table II sets out the performance of various investments, had they been made immediately following that announcement which brought a *de jure* end to the "good-as-gold" dollar and a *de facto* end to the Bretton Woods System.

TABLE II

	Gold	Silver	Swiss Franc*	D.J.I.A.**	$Dep.a/c at 6%***
Aug. 15, 1971	$ 43.00	$ 1.59	.2462	889.0	$1,000.
Mar. 21, 1980	$525.00	$21.01	.5634	785.15	$1,663.
Change	+1120%	+1221%	+129%	-12%	+66%

*Ignores interest earnings. **Ignores dividend yield. ***Pre-tax.

The Third Major Confirmation of runaway and uncontrollable inflation came in February of 1973 when once again, following on the heels of a massive and new record balance-of-payments deficit and soaring inflation rates in the U.S., currency markets virtually ground to a halt in chaos and the dollar was again devalued, this time by 10 percent. The fixed exchange rate system was completely abandoned and officially sanctioned "floating" rates resulted. ERC again urged investment funds be moved into silver, gold and Swiss francs.

Table III illustrates the performance of investments if they had been made on February 13, 1973, when the U.S. again devalued the dollar.

TABLE III

	Gold	Silver	Swiss Franc*	D.J.I.A.**	$ Dep. a/c at 6%***
Feb. 13, 1973	$ 68.90	$ 2.19	.3000	996.70	$1,000.
Mar. 21, 1980	$525.00	$21.01	.5634	785.15	$1,522.
Change	+662%	+859%	+88%	-21%	+52%

*Ignores interest earnings. **Ignores dividend yield. ***Pre-tax.

Once again, as the table illustrates, gold, silver and Swiss franc deposits significantly outperformed the other investments.

In April, 1977, we warned that a renewed dollar crisis much like '73 - '74 could be expected to emerge in the second half of 1977. Gold was then at $149.50, silver, $4.85, the Swiss franc, 39.6 U.S. cents, and the D.J.I.A. at 943. Then in October 1977, when gold was slightly up at $154, silver slightly down at $4.64 and the Swiss franc up 8 percent at 42.9 cents, we observed that under floating rates (between currencies), "governments do not announce a devaluation on a given day; instead, the markets do, over a period of weeks and months." We said further that . .".*The Fourth Signal* of renewed decline in the dollar, and. . .rise in recommended hard-money investments may well be emerging in the markets now" and we advised that additional funds be committed to these recommended positions. Table IV shows the results to-date for those who acted on that recommendation.

TABLE IV

	Gold	Silver	Platinum	Swiss Franc*	D.J.I.A.**	$ Dep. a/c at 6%***
August 20, 1977			$146.00			
October 7, 1977	$153.95	$ 4.64		.4292	840.3	$1,000.
March 21, 1980	$525.00	$21.01	$630.00	.5634	785.15	$1,166.
Change	+241%	+353%	+331%	+31%	6%	+17%

*Ignores interest earnings. **Ignores dividend yield. ***Pre-tax.

The January 1979 (annual forecast) issue of *World Market Perspective* predicted that 1979 would see "a stronger dollar, booming markets, no recession." This outlook was completely at odds with the generally held view that 1979 would usher in recessionary times. The following quotation from that issue sums up part of the reasoning behind the accurate predictions:

> The dollar will strengthen in 1979, relative to other currencies, primarily because of the tax-revolt-induced sharp slowdown in the expansion of destructive government and because the 1978 dollar plunge against the European and Japanese currencies, especially the Swiss franc, was to a large extent an emotional, speculative over-reaction which pushed the dollar far lower in relation to other currencies then underlying economic factors warranted.
>
> At the same time, with market focus on foreign exchange rates fluctuations, the markets in 1978 did not discount currency values generally against the precious metals as much as fundamental factors (particularly currency inflation rates) warranted. Hence, the conclusion and prediction that, in 1979, the dollar will strengthen against other currencies, particularly the Swiss franc, while gold, silver and platinum will move to new highs in terms of all of the national paper currencies — particularly against the recent heavily inflated Swiss franc.

Throughout 1979, events in the marketplace provided evidence that a *Fifth Signal* of runaway inflation was being flashed. Precious metal prices broke into new high ground not only against the U.S. dollar but also in terms of the Swiss franc, the West German mark and the Japanese yen.

Table V shows the results to-date for those who acted on the recommendations of the January issue of *World Market Perspective*, the strongest of which was to buy silver.

TABLE V

	Gold	Silver	Platinum	Swiss Franc*	D.J.I.A.**	Dep. a/c at 6%***
January 16, 1979	$220.65	$ 6.03	$354.00	.5900	835.59	$1,000.
March 21, 1980	$525.00	$21.01	$630.00	.5634	785.15	$1,075.90
Change	+138%	+248%	+78%	-4.5%	-6%	+7.6%

*Ignores interest earnings. **Ignores dividend yield. ***Pre-tax.

Now, in the second quarter of 1980, all of ERC's recommended investments are declining, responding to the fact that the credit cycle has peaked (as we warned in the March 1980 issue of the *Perspective*), and to growing recessionary psychology, and are approaching the bottom of a significant period of price decline within their ongoing long-term uptrends.

Even in such virulent inflationary experiences as that which wracked the German economy following World War I, periods of disinflation and price moderation occurred. They are to be expected and such periods provide a golden opportunity for those individuals who have not acted previously to begin the orderly establishment of precious metal portfolios that will protect them during the succeeding inevitable waves of runaway inflation and eventual hyperinflation.

In the decade of the 1970s there were three clear and unequivocal official signals and two market-action signals that the foundations of our monetary and economic system are under an unrelenting and unrestrained attack by the very officials who are supposed to preserve them. Each time, defensive "hard money" investments paid off, as they will in the future during new attacks in the ongoing war against the dollar.

A Word of Caution

Many will read this book months after it has been prepared. Market conditions, especially short-term factors, change, sometimes frequently and sometimes markedly. We would caution all readers not to take action on any of the conclusions of this book without first obtaining current market information and analysis. This is easily done: all recommendations are reviewed in light of current conditions in each monthly issue of *World Market Perspective*. Further, Economic Research Counselors (ERC) is available by toll-free telephone (800-426-5270) to assist readers personally.

APPENDIX II

U.S. Currency Controls

Under the presumed authority of Public Law 91-508, the United States Treasury has removed your freedom to transfer amounts of $5,000 or more abroad *without reporting the details* of your transactions to the United States Treasury.

The regulations do not prohibit such transfers. Strictly speaking these regulations, so far, are reporting requirements and not currency controls. * However, it appears obvious that this is but a first step towards outright currency controls prohibiting such transfers except with official permission. It is also obvious that anyone contemplating a transfer of funds abroad in any amount would be wise to make the transfer ahead of the imposition of full controls. Once embarked on a program of currency controls, the government can gradually reduce the amounts to $2,500 then to $1,000 on down to $500 with all kinds of restrictions as to what amounts travelers can take out of the country, combined with onerous controls upon exports, imports and commerce in general.

Moderate controls have a moderate effect and cause recessions, but they don't even slow down speculative currency flows (often, by the alarm they create, scared money flight is increased). Seeing such results, officialdom considers it a *necessity* to apply severe controls. Severe controls have severe effects; they cause depression. This is the direction in which we are headed — a repeat of the early 1930s.

For individuals, the major requirements of P.L.91-508 are that they:

(1) Cannot physically take more than $5,000 in U.S. currency, foreign currency, travelers' checks, money orders or bearer-form negotiable securities out of the country without submitting a new Internal Revenue Service Form 4790 to the customs officer on the spot.

Barron's has described these rules as "exchange controls by intimidation."

161

(2) Must file the same form when arriving in the U.S. with such a sum. If the money is mailed or otherwise transported separately, the form must be mailed to the Customs Commissioner in Washington by the date the money moves in or out. A person receiving such money unreported by the sender has 30 days to mail a form to a local customs office or to Washington. This reporting is also required of anyone arranging such a physical movement of monetary instruments in or out of the country; it doesn't apply to transfer through banking channels.

(3) Must keep records for five years on the maximum amount and other aspects of any foreign bank account they may have, and continue under more specific legal authority to report the existence of such an account on income tax returns.

Legally the terms "Money," "Currency" and "Monetary Instruments" do not include cashier's checks made payable to the order of a named person which bear a restrictive endorsement (e.g., "For deposit to. . . "). The applicable rules and regulations, published in the Federal Register, Vol. 37, No. 66, April 5th, 1972, define currency and monetary instruments thus: **Currency** — "The coin and currency of the United States or of any other country . . . *does not include bank checks or other negotiable instruments not customarily accepted as money.*" **Monetary Instrument** — "Coin or currency . . . travelers' checks, money orders, investment securities bearer form . . . *the term does not include bank checks made payable to the order of a named person which have not been endorsed or which bear restrictive endorsements . . . A transaction which is a transfer of funds by means of bank check, bank draft, wire transfer, or other written order, and which does not include the physical transfer of currency is not a transaction in currency . . . .*"

The major impact on banks and other financial institutions is that they have to keep certain records longer than they otherwise would. The financial institutions also have to report unusual currency transactions— domestic or foreign — of more than $5,000 each, retain records of all transfers of more than $5,000 into or out of the U.S. for five years, and keep certain other records for five years. In addition, banks have to keep for two years "records which would be needed to reconstruct a deposit or share account and to trace a check in excess of $100 deposited in such an account . . ." Similarly, a bank must keep for five years a microfilm or other copy of each such check drawn on it.

These regulations, however, are subject to change at the whim of the Secretary of the Treasury — limited only by the very broad powers contained in the law itself. The principal requirements of this law as it affects individuals are set forth on the following pages.

This entire law speaks eloquently for itself. To any thinking person it would seem obvious that its authoritarian provisions are in direct violation of the constitutional guarantee of privacy. Still, under our legal system as it is administered today, one must spend many, many thousands of dollars and many months to establish judicially the unconstitutionality of such a law.

Until that is done, the only prudent course for anyone wishing to avoid entanglement with the federal government, and possible future exposure to criminal and civil penalties, is to observe one or more of the following precautions:

(1) Make all transfers of actual cash (i.e., currency, travelers' checks, money orders or any bearer-form securities) only in amounts of less than $5,000 each;

(2) Whenever possible, convert funds into a cashier's check made payable to yourself and restrictively endorsed with "For Deposit To My Account Only" ahead of your signature; and/or,

(3) When speed is important, or when the amount is large, make the transfer(s) by bank wire through normal banking channels (if you wish to avoid the bank making a report of your transactions to the U.S. Treasury).

Domestic Currency Transactions

§ 221. *Reports of currency transactions required*

Transactions involving any domestic financial institution shall be reported to the Secretary at such time, in such a manner, and in such detail as the Secretary may require if they involve the payment, receipt, or transfer of United States currency, or such other monetary instruments as the Secretary may specify, in such amounts, denominations, or both, or under such circumstances, as the Secretary shall by regulation prescribe.

§ 222. *Persons required to file reports*

The report of any transaction required to be reported under this chapter shall be signed or otherwise made both by the domestic financial institution involved and by one or more of the other parties thereto or participants therein, as the Secretary may require. If any party to or participant in the transaction is not an individual acting only for himself, the report shall identify the person or persons on whose behalf the transaction is entered into, and shall be made by the individuals acting as agents or bailees with respect thereto.

§ 223. *Reporting procedure*

(a) The Secretary may in his discretion designate domestic financial institutions, individually or by class, as agents of the United States to receive reports required under this chapter, . . .

(b) Any person (other than an institution designated under subsection (a)) required to file a report under this chapter with respect to a transaction with a domestic financial institution shall file the report with that institution, except that (1) if the institution is not designated under subsection (a), the report shall be filed as the Secretary shall prescribe, and (2) any such person may, at his election and in lieu of filing the report in the manner herein above prescribed, file the report with the Secretary. Domestic financial institutions designated under subsection (a) shall transmit reports filed with them, and shall file their own reports, as the Secretary shall prescribe.

International Currency Transactions

§ 231. *Reports*

(a) Except as provided in subsection (c) of this section, whoever, whether as principal, agent, or bailee, or by an agent or bailee, knowingly —

(1) transports or causes to be transported monetary instruments —

(A) from any place within the United States or through any place outside the United States, or

(B) to any place within the United States from or through any place outside the United States, or

(2) receives monetary instruments at the termination of their transportation to the United States from or through any place outside the United States in *an amount exceeding $5,000 on any one occasion* shall file a report or reports in accordance with subsection (b) of this section.

(b) Reports required under this section shall be filed at such times and places, and may contain such of the following information and any additional information, in such form and in such detail, as the Secretary may require:

(1) The legal capacity in which the person filing the report is acting with respect to the monetary instruments transported.

(2) The origin, destination, and route of the transportation.

(3) Where the monetary instruments are not legally and beneficially owned by the person transporting the same, or are transported for any purpose other than the use in his own behalf of the person transporting the same, the identities of the person from whom the monetary instruments are received, or to whom they are to be delivered, or both.

(4) The amounts and types of monetary instruments transported.

§ 232. *Forfeiture*

(a) Any monetary instruments which are in the process of any transportation with respect to which any report required to be filed under section 231 (1) either has not been filed or contains material omissions or misstatements are subject to seizure and forfeiture to the United States.

(b) For the purpose of this section, monetary instruments transported by Mail, by any common carrier, or by any messenger or bailee, are in process of transportation from the time they are delivered into the possession of the postal service, common carrier, messenger, or bailee . . .

§ 241. *Records and reports*

(a) The Secretary of the Treasury, having due regard for the need to avoid impeding or controlling the export or import of currency or other monetary instruments and having due regard also for the need to avoid burdening unreasonably persons who legitimately engage in transactions with foreign financial agencies, shall by regulation require any resident or citizen of the United States, or person in the United States and doing business therein, who engages in any transaction or maintains any relationship, directly or indirectly, on behalf of himself or another, with a foreign financial agency to maintain records or to file reports, or both, setting forth such of the following information, in such form and in such detail, as the Secretary may require:

(1) The identities and addresses of the parties to the transaction or relationship.

(2) The legal capacities in which the parties to the transaction or relationship are acting, and the identities of the real parties in interest if one or more of the parties are not acting solely as principals.

(3) A description of the transaction or relationship including the amounts of money, credit, or other property involved.

(b) No person required to maintain records under this section shall be required to produce or otherwise disclose the contents of the records except in compliance with a subpoena or summons duly authorized and issued or as may otherwise be required by law.

§ 242. *Classifications and requirements*
The Secretary may prescribe:

(1) Any reasonable classification of persons subject to or exempt from any requirement imposed under section 241.

(2) The foreign country or countries as to which any requirement imposed under section 241 applies or does not apply if, in the judgement of the Secretary, uniform applicability of any such requirement to all foreign countries is unnecessary or undesirable.

(3) The magnitude of transactions subject to any requirement imposed under section 241.

(4) Types of transactions subject to or exempt from any requirement imposed under section 241.

(5) Such other matters as he may deem necessary to the application of this chapter.

Appendix III

Lessons from History on Official Paper Money Inflation

Lesson One: Medieval China*

During the roughly 6,000 years of recorded history, there have been 34 discernible civilizations.** Of all these, only two used paper money. We are all too familiar with the experience of one of these civilizations: our own. But Western civilization was not the first. Western eyes first saw the Chinese using paper and printing presses, and Marco Polo included paper money along with spaghetti, gunpowder, and porcelain in his tales of wondrous Chinese inventions.

Modern paper (as opposed to Egyptian papyrus) was invented in about 50 B.C. Short lengths of bamboo were beaten into pulp, formed into sheets and dried. This method is very close to modern techniques.

The history of paper money in China stretches over seven dynasties and some 800 years; it dates from the ninth century to the seventeenth. Eight times the Chinese tried systems of unbacked paper currencies. Eight times the fiat was abandoned; several times only after the value had plummeted to zero. Often, collapse of the "official" currency was followed by a proliferation of private currencies.

The origins of Chinese paper money have a familiar ring:

*Excerpted from *Swiss Economic Viewpoint*, Oct. 1, 1976 . Published quarterly by Foreign Commerce Bank, Bellariastrasse 82, 8038 Zurich, Switzerland.

**These are documented in Arnold Toynbee's monumental 12-volume series, *A Study of History*.

167

About 700 A.D. people first began to take valuables to merchants who stored them and issued receipts to owners. By 1000 A.D. these merchants discovered that the receipts themselves circulated as money, and began issuing more notes than the amount of valuables they had on deposit.

Soon afterwards the Sung conquered most of China and entered this profitable storage business. These rulers issued paper money during the next century, but they did it modestly and gradually, giving the people time to get used to it. This gradual introduction made the future fiat money possible for people to accept, in like manner to modern experience.* Meanwhile another part of China was indeed using unbacked paper. Paper money probably developed faster in Szechuan province because the metal it replaced was iron, too cumbersome for ready use. At first a fixed quota of currency was annually printed for redemption in new notes three years later. This stable currency system became the Chinese equivalent of the gold standard, and for a century it prevented the government from inflating. But in 1072 a second series of 1071 notes was run off. The yearly issues got larger and soon redemption dates were frequently missed. In 35 years the money supply rose 2,000 percent. Not long afterward the currency passed out of use.

By this time a new dynasty, the Southern Sung, had replaced the Sung in the rest of China. Several unsuccessful attempts were made to get paper established; this finally succeeded in 1168. The same "three-year plan" was inaugurated, with a quota of 10 million "strings" a year. The "string" was the Chinese paper currency. Just as the English pound began as a pound of sterling silver, the string represented an actual string upon which a thousand copper coins had been threaded. (This custom is the reason for the hole in the middle of Chinese coins.)

*This sort of lengthy introduction is often necessary; the following incident illustrates it: Three centuries later, the Chinese conquered Persia and tried to introduce the same fiat money being used back in Peking. Advisers and presses were duly sent, but the Persians had never before seen paper money. They simply refused to believe that the nicely printed pieces of paper were worth anything. The experiment failed.

Deficit spending soon caused the government to inflate. In 1176 certain issues were allowed to circulate nine years instead of three. In 1195 the yearly quota was tripled; and by 1209 the money supply was twenty times its original size. Until this time, however, the paper's value held firm. This could be explained by the fact that the paper gradually made its way to the outlying provinces of the empire. Eventually the point was reached where paper circulated throughout the whole empire, and any further increase would cause depreciation. This dangerous point was reached about 1210. The Southern Sung chose this moment to launch a war against the barbarian Chin* dynasty to the north. The war failed and the value of Sung paper plummeted. By 1232 the money supply had tripled and soon periods of circulation became unlimited. The currency began to be printed on silky paper infused with a delicate hint of perfume, to make it more attractive, but this tactic fooled no one. Not long afterward, the Mongols conquered the Sung.

Meanwhile, the Chin were also issuing paper currency. The Chin currency was remarkable in that there were separate issues for the various geographical areas under their control. Depreciation, as usual, began slowly. But for the first time in Chinese history, various laws were passed to stem too rapid a fall. For instance, in 1192 an imperial decree prevented the paper supply from exceeding the copper supply. The next year certain taxes were ordered paid in paper, thus increasing the demand for it. But copper began to be hoarded, and silver was introduced at par with paper to draw attention away from copper. Both silver and paper were highly overvalued against copper, and were ignored. A measure was enacted that every transaction involving over one string had to be made in notes or (while it lasted) silver. This would be the first in an increasing number of actions during the next centuries designed to eliminate monies competing with official fiat. In 1206, a particularly ludicrous anti-inflationary technique was employed. Efforts were made to withdraw the largest denomination bills, because they were somehow considered more inflationary

*For whom China is named.

than, say, two or three smaller bills totalling the same amount. (This belief seems to be endemic in China, for the same phenomenon was observed in the post-World War II Chinese inflation.)

The steady use of the printing press rendered all these measures useless. And the above-mentioned war with the Southern Sung was also a blow to the Chin currency. In addition, the Mongols began to menace Chin frontiers. Due to high military spending, currency values rapidly disintegrated. Eighty-four cartloads of paper were distributed to the troops just before a severe Chin defeat (1210). The rulers began issuing notes of ever-increasing denomination, apparently realizing the foolishness of the 1206 edict. There was a brief, unsuccessful experiment in price controls. New issues became worthless practically overnight, and by 1216 they were worth less than one percent of their face value. The next year a "new" currency was issued at the rate of 1,000 to one. It wasn't enough: a newer currency (1222) replaced it at an 800-to-one rate (its current "black market" value). Before the year had passed this sank below one percent of face value. Soon after, both the Chin government and its currency were put out of their miseries by the Mongol hordes of Genghis Khan.

Remarkably, the Mongols did not at first consider the possibilities of paper money. But in 1260 Kublai Khan made a former Chin inflationist his principal advisor. The presses began rolling in that year, and were to cease only with the demise of Mongol rule. A national currency was issued, but began to lose value instantly. Accordingly, for the only time in history, that value was legally set at one-half face value. Initially, currency value was maintained. The Mongols had an empire much larger than the Sung, so years elapsed before new money brought price inflation. In 1262 a series of very tough decrees began. Gold and silver were prohibited in exchange, the penalty being death. (It seems that the Mongol penalty for most crimes was death, but then a regime which several times seriously considered a policy of killing *all* Chinese and turning China into pasture land could not be expected to feel remorse in enacting severe punishments for even minor infractions.)

Between 1260 and 1330 the monetary inflation rate was an incredible *323,300 percent*, an average of over *4,600 percent* a year!* This seventy-year period was characterized by numerous issues of new paper currency, and continual decrees to enforce its acceptance. Refusal to accept notes in exchange brought death to "only" the offender, but counterfeiting them brought death to three generations!

It was at this time that Marco Polo visited China. He waxed enthusiastic about the glories of paper money: "Each year," he said, the Great Khan "has so great a supply of them (notes) made in Peking that he could buy with it all the treasure in the world, though it costs him nothing."

Polo seemed unaware of any problems the fiat caused. Indeed, he never even mentioned the yearly decline of its value all the while he was in China. He brought this rose-colored picture back to Europe, and doubtless swayed future generations. Private currencies began to compete with government money to such an extent that in 1294 their use was outlawed. These private monies were tokens issued by reputable commercial establishments entitling the bearer to various commodities of general usefulness, such as a pound of salt. While the decrees against private money worked fairly well in large cities, they failed utterly in the vast outlying districts.

Dogged by catastrophe on both the international and home fronts, the Mongol empire began to disintegrate. As a result of increasing disorder, most statistical data ends in 1330. We do know that by 1350 people valued only hard cash. The dynasty ended in 1368. The Mings, who conquered them, were just as inflationary during and after their successful uprising. But once again, currency initially held its value. However, by 1400 the notes had fallen to three percent of face value, by 1425 to one percent, and by 1450 to one-tenth of one percent.

Inflation Finally Halted

But the Mings had learned their lesson and gradually stopped printing money, rapidly replacing it with metal coins. From 1500 on we hear little of Chinese paper money. The

*From 360,000 strings in 1260 to 116.4 billion in 1330.

Mings briefly considered using it just before they fell to the Manchus in 1644, and the new dynasty only fleetingly printed money (1650-1661). In fact, China did not use paper again until it was introduced in 1851 by the British, the Western descendants of Marco Polo, the man who brought the inventions of paper and printing back home with him.

While the *government* had stopped using paper money, private merchants again began issuing notes after 1500. With centuries of inflation behind them, most merchants shunned note over-issue. (The public put those who didn't out of business.) Different commodities were used by different note issuers; some notes were backed, for instance, by bricks of tea.

Conclusion

Certainly the most interesting feature of this Chinese monetary history is that, after 500 years' experience, China eventually abandoned state-sponsored paper money in favor of hard money and private banknotes. Western use of government fiat money has run only about 250 years. Let us hope we don't wait another 250 years to repudiate it before we repeat medieval China's ultimate act of sanity.

Lesson Two: France, 1790-96*

It is easy to forget the perils of inflation when things seem to be going smoothly and when the government keeps assuring us there is nothing to worry about.

But the mounting alarm of economists and bankers (even Chairman Martin of the federal reserve board fears we are on the brink of a new inflation) should alert us to the havoc that inflation can cause — and has caused in one country after another. We mustn't become so anesthetized by the promises of a government financed utopia as to forget that other countries have tumbled over the brink in pursuit of the same enticing goal. And the government's mechanical assurances should remind us of similar assurances which have been given so often before, and have proved false.

They should remind us that in 1790, on the eve of the great classic example of inflation, members of the revolutionary French national assembly welcomed the proposal to restore prosperity by issuing paper money, called "assignats," backed by the land which had been seized from the church. It was hailed as "the only means to insure happiness, glory, and liberty to the French nation."

"We are told," the respected nobleman, Mirabeau, informed the assembly, "that paper money will become superabundant. Of what paper do you speak? If of a paper without a solid base, undoubtedly; if of one based on the firm foundation of landed property, never."

Of course Mirabeau knew better; barely a year earlier he had denounced paper money as "a nursery of tyranny, corruption, and delusion." But France faced a financial crisis, and in time of crisis even intelligent men sometimes grasp for the most convenient straws.

The tragedy of the assignats is well known. At first, the issue was limited to 400 million livres, and was used to pay pressing government obligations. The assignats could be used to buy

*Lessons 2 through 6 are excerpted from *Reminders of Inflation*, a series of articles on inflation published by the *Chicago Tribune*, March 14-18, 1965.

In 1796, the French national currency, the assignat, was hyperinflated to destruction. The assignats were burned in great quantities throughout France by a people weary of fiat money inflation. Distrust of paper money continues in France to the present day.

the church land, in which event they were to be retired from circulation, or they could continue in circulation as long as land was available as security.

But as the land was sold, the government failed to destroy

the money. It spent it over again; and as still more money was
needed to prepare for war and to keep the people content, it
printed new assignats.

Prices rose daily. When Queen Marie Antoinette was told
the people couldn't afford bread, she is said to have suggested
they eat cake. Instead of pacifying the people, the outpouring
of assignats angered them. Moderate leaders were replaced by
radicals; the royal family was guillotined, and the assignats
were pumped out faster than ever. Soon the peasants refused
to accept paper money, complaining it couldn't be used even
to feed the horses. A loaf of bread cost 45 livres, or what had
been almost a year's wages. By 1796, it took 12,000 paper
livres to buy the gold louis, a coin which had once been the
equivalent of one livre. Only half of the former church lands
remained as security for the assignats, but their volume had
climbed to 45 ½ billion livres.

In the fall of 1795, citizens of Paris rebelled and a 26-year-
old artillery officer named Napoleon Bonaparte subdued them
with "a whiff of grapeshot."

The assignats were abandoned in 1796, but the economy remained in disarray and four years later the Directory was
dismissed by the same Napoleon, who established a new
money system and in 1800 turned the responsibility for paper
money over to the new and autonomous Bank of France.

The bank remained independent until the end of 1945,
when a socialistic government took it over and plunged the
country into financial chaos once again.

Lesson Three:
Weimar Germany, 1922-23

A Swedish traveler walked into the largest bank in Wurttemberg, Germany, in 1923 and asked to change 100 Swedish kroner into marks. The cashier apologized that the bank had only 20 million marks on hand and could, therefore, make change for only eight kroner. Germans waiting in line behind the Swede begged him not to take all the bank's money. The mark was losing value so fast, they said, that if they couldn't cash their pay checks and spend the money immediately, it would buy only half as much food the next day. The Swede took change for two kroner (52 cents in our money) and left.

This is just one of countless published stories about the most extreme case of inflation in history. Although the German government was only partly to blame for the chaos, the experience shows how runaway inflation can wipe out the savings of half the citizenry and can create the conditions in which a Hitler could thrive.

Financially, Germany was not much worse off at the end of World War I than its neighbors. The Reichsbank had suspended payments in gold so as to enable the government to expand the supply of paper money and pay for the war. By 1919, the mark was down to about 12 cents, half its pre-war value — but the same was true of the franc and other currencies.

It was the allies who set the stage for the collapse of the mark by imposing limits on German industry in 1919, and in 1921 by handing Germany an impossible reparations bill (for 132 billion gold marks) and giving half of the Upper Silesian industrial area to Poland.

With Germany in this straitjacket, pessimists there and abroad began to get rid of their marks, and by November, 1921, the foreign exchange value of the mark was down to one-third of a cent. But as yet there was little inflation of the money supply within Germany, and the storm of pessimism might have been weathered if the German government had been willing and able to balance its budget and thus avoid putting any more marks into circulation. This it failed to do, partly because it was an inexperienced, left-wing regime without the will to hold down spending, and partly because a vindictive France refused to grant a moratorium on the reparations, even though Britain and Italy were willing.

Any hope that was left for the mark in late 1922 was dashed in January, 1923, when French troops moved into the Ruhr industrial area and set up what Premier Poincare called a "mission of control" to squeeze the reparations money out of German industry.

The Germans replied with passive resistance. They closed the factories, and the Berlin government ground out billions of new marks, largely to support the resistance. As prices went up, the billions became trillions and the trillions became quadrillions. Two thousand printing presses enlisted by the Reichsbank could not keep up with the demand for money. In the nine months following the occupation of the Ruhr, the mark fell from 20,000 to 4.2 trillion to the dollar. In November there were more than 518 quintillion marks in circulation.

Housewives lucky enough to get money had to carry it in satchels. An egg which had cost a quarter of a mark in 1918 cost 5,000 marks in the summer of 1923 and 80 billion in November. Very few people would lend money, even at the going rate of 20 percent a day — though the Reichsbank continued to accept IOUs from government and industry at a mere 90 percent a year, and print paper money for them in return.

In early 1923, Berlin railroad workers went on strike for an increase in their weekly 2 ½ million mark wages. After three days they settled for 9 million a week. And by the end of the first week the 9 million wouldn't buy as much as the 2 ½ million had bought when they went on strike. Shops would close at intervals during the day in order that new prices could be posted. Street car fares went up daily.

Hughston McBain, the Chicago merchant, happened to be in Berlin in the fall of 1922 and wrote of being able to treat his German friends to luxuries which they couldn't dream of buying for themselves for only a few cents in American money.

In November, 1923, the nightmare came to an end with the

issuance of new "rentenmarks,"one for each trillion inflation marks. The rentenmark was backed in theory by the land of the country and was thus no sounder in principle than the old French assignats; it worked only because the government refused to increase the supply and because the people knew that it had to work.

But it was too late to save the middle class — the townspeople living on fixed incomes from salaries, pensions, interests, or rent. Until late in 1923, courts enforced the right of debtors to pay off their debts in the worthless marks. People who once had lived comfortably on the income from bonds or mortgages found themselves paid off in full for less than the cost of a cup of coffee. They were reduced to selling their furniture and clothing in order to buy food to live, and many chose suicide instead.

Those who survived were glad to listen to the promises of the National Socialists, who were busy in Berlin as early as 1919. And thus the inflation resulting from one war created conditions which helped to bring about the next.

Lesson Four: Italy and Poland

Like nearly all modern wars, World War II ushered in a period of inflation which, in many places, is still going on. But it would be misleading to say that war creates inflation. War creates conditions in which inflation thrives — an abundance of money and a shortage of consumer goods — but this doesn't make inflation inevitable.

It is significant, for example, that the two countries which were hardest hit by inflation after World War I — Germany and Russia — were among the least affected after World War II even though their physical destruction had been greater than in the first war.

They had learned their lesson the hard way. When a team of American economists handed Germany an inflationary prescription shortly after the end of the war, the Germans filed it away and proceeded in the opposite direction — with conspicuous success. Previously, in 1948, the Germans had countered the threat of inflation by reforming the currency and issuing only enough new Deutsche marks to conform to the supply of goods available. The effect of this was to hold prices steady and force people to work and produce more if they wanted to buy more.

Where inflation did occur, as in Italy, Poland, and France, it was not so much because of the war as because of the policies of socialistic post-war governments which made the familiar mistake of assuming that more government controls and more spending would mean more prosperity.

Italy had experienced some inflation after World War I (enough, in fact, to help make a success of Mussolini's march on Rome in 1922); but when things settled down, prices leveled off at from four to seven times what they had been in 1914 and a disaster like Germany's was averted.

Therefore when Italy turned to the socialists again after Mussolini's downfall, the people were eager to believe the promises of socialism and to overlook what had happened 20 years before in Germany — if indeed they knew of it. The government embarked on a program of nationalization and welfarism which has kept it in the red almost constantly ever since. The best that can be said of today's deficits is that they are not as bad as in 1949, when the government spent almost twice what it took in.

An inflated wartime money supply was further inflated by government programs designed to help those who were not working and by an endless succession of pay raises for the burgeoning army of government payrollers who weren't producing anything of value. Prices inevitably soared; by 1949 the lira would buy barely one-fiftieth of what it would buy in 1938. It dropped from 20 to the dollar to 640. And as prices rose, a familiar reaction set in; people demanded higher pay and more handouts instead of greater production. Industrial workers were more interested in striking than in working. The incentive to work which Germany had created was missing.

As prices went up, it was possible in one case for a man to embezzle 5 million lire from his employer, get caught, repay the money plus a sizable fine, and still come out ahead. He was a prudent thief. He had used the loot to invest in property and on being caught he sold it for double what he had paid for it.

But most people were much less fortunate, especially the landlords. While their costs doubled and redoubled, their rental income was frozen. Tenants of large and luxurious apartments would stay on and on, long after their children had married and moved away, because as long as they remained, their rent was trivial; if they moved to a smaller apartment without a rent ceiling, they would have paid four or five times as much. Thus the housing shortage was aggravated.

Pensioners and others with fixed incomes added to the pressure for government handouts, thus increasing the money supply by another round and adding nothing to the supply of purchasable goods. Marshall plan aid helped, to the extent that it went into production; but the extravagances and the deficits continue, and Italian prices are still rising.

Behind the iron curtain socialism produced the same results. Glorious things were promised by the Communists when they took over the Polish government and, in 1948, tied the zloty to the Russian ruble instead of the dollar. But efforts to communize the farms soon boomeranged; food production plummeted and prices rose until in 1957 Poland found it was unable to obtain any more western money except by admitting that the zloty had declined in value from 25 cents to 4 cents, and offering it to the west at that price.

It may still be asked how Russia, the champion socialist state of all, managed to avoid so common a pitfall of socialism. Thomas Wilson, a British economist, gives the answer in his recent book, *Inflation*. Russian workers can't strike for higher pay, they can't quit their jobs, Russian voters can't force the government to give them handouts, and the Russian people, lacking a free press, were so ignorant they they didn't even know what was bad for them. The Russian government, fearing inflation, manipulated the money system so as to avoid it. Russia succeeded, but its method will hardly appeal to free men.

Lesson Five: Post-War France

When Napoleon Bonaparte entrusted the French money system to the new and independent Bank of France in 1800 after the collapse of the Revolutionary assignats, he declared that he would never allow France to be defrauded again by irredeemable paper money.

But a lesson learned, no matter how painful the experience, rarely seems to last more than a lifetime. Later generations have to relearn it for themselves. And one of the first things the socialists under Leon Blum did in December, 1945, when they dominated the provisional de Gaulle government, was to nationalize the Bank of France and thus, in effect, put the money supply in the hands of the politicians. De Gaulle resigned the following month, and Blum soon became premier.

Instead of limiting the money supply and encouraging production, as Germany was to do in 1948, the French Socialists interfered with production by taking over large segments of industry, and they pumped up the money supply by a succession of vast government deficits. Deliberate deficits caused by socialistic welfare spending were augmented by emergency deficits caused by the fighting in Indo-China and later in Algeria. The military spending was budgeted separately, as if a deficit caused by emergency military spending was, somehow, different from one caused by welfare programs. But unfortunately inflation doesn't know one from the other.

As deficit after deficit was financed by "printing press" money, the volume of currency in circulation climbed from 500 billion francs in 1945 to 868 billion in 1947, 1,886 billion in 1952, and 3,500 billion in 1957, when a degree of stability was finally restored.

The bank had long since stopped redeeming money in gold. The franc, which emerged from the war at about half of its pre-war value, or two cents, fell to less than one cent by the end of 1945. Successive governments tried to forestall nature by all sorts of regulations and controls, but in vain. For every regulation there was a bribe, and for every control a loophole. It was as impossible to legislate a stable franc in the 1940s and

1950s as it had been in the 1790s, when it was made a capital offense to dispose of a paper assignat at less than face value. One after another, a procession of governments promised to stabilize the franc, and one after another they refused to follow through with the economy and discipline which were necessary to do the job.

The black market value of the franc fell to 480 to the dollar in 1952. Prices in 1946 were five times those of 1938; in 1949 they were 15 times as high and in 1953 20 times as high.

Production, already handicapped by government controls, was further stalled by strikes; and the successive government crises made it impossible to know what the government was going to do from month to month. There were occasional and unrealistic proposals to levy a confiscatory tax on business or the wealthy, but most of them came to nothing. The property owners protected themselves by buying gold, when they could get it, and by buying foreign land and securities.

Marshall plan aid is credited with helping to revive French industry, and no doubt it did. But the amount received through the Marshall plan — about 5 billion dollars — was only half the amount which would have been available right in France if inflation and an irresponsible government hadn't driven it into hiding. Jacques Rueff, the economist, reported to Gen. de Gaulle in 1958 that the French people had stashed away about 10 billion dollars.

With almost no gold available to back paper money or to guarantee loans, it was difficult for the government or anybody else to borrow money. Antoine Pinay overcame this problem in 1952, as finance minister, by issuing rubber bonds, repayable not in the number of francs borrowed, but in the number which would buy the same amount of gold if gold could be bought. This worked until lenders realized the official value of the franc in relation to gold was arbitrary and fictitious and set to favor the borrowers, including the government.

So they insisted that the amount of repayment be determined by more realistic measures such as the price of wheat, electricity, or cement. Similar escalator clauses were built into wage contracts. Farm leases were stated in terms of butter or milk. And a country doctor's fee for an office call might be the current price of a chicken.

As is always true of inflation, it was the pensioners, small property owners, and middle class townspeople who suffered the most. A typical example is the Frenchman who retired in the late 1930s as regional manager for a Chicago firm. When he retired, he had a comfortable income from insurance, pension, and interest on a savings account. Today his life savings barely yield enough, as he puts it, for two good meals at Maxim's.

"I was taken in," he confesses, "by the representations of the government that the franc would always be good."

And having been deluded by the government, he finds himself now largely dependent on it.

Lesson Six: Brazil

Germany, Russia, France, and Italy have demonstrated how a socialistic or irresponsible government can plunge a country into ruinous inflation with the help of a war. Brazil, for one, has shown us how such a government can do just as thorough a job without any help at all.

Brazil has been in financial trouble more or less chronically since the overthrow of the empire in 1889. A succession of inexperienced and visionary governments created such chaos that for years they had to keep one set of books in terms of the gold milreis and another in terms of the paper milreis, which was worth a great deal less.

But in the late 1920s a certain amount of order was restored and the milreis leveled off at 5 or 6 cents in our money. World War II had little effect on it, although the name was changed to cruzeiro in order to distinguish it from the former Portuguese coin.

Brazil's previous financial difficulties have been dwarfed in the last decade or so, and the trouble began as a result of conditions which should sound very familiar to Americans today: a foreign exchange deficit and persistent demands for increased domestic spending.

The foreign exchange trouble came about, ironically, because of the high price of coffee in the years immediately following 1950. American housewives refused to buy Brazilian coffee, and Brazil's dollar income fell off sharply. Meanwhile, many Brazilians, and especially the increasingly powerful Socialists, were clamoring for wage increases, expansion of government activity, and the development by the government of new industries, especially oil. The problem was how to spend money that didn't exist, and even before the Socialists came to power in 1956, the government had invented an intricate sort of shell game by which it could feed IOUs into one door of the government-owned Bank of Brazil and receive brand-new paper money out of another door, while at the same time pretending that it wasn't creating new money at all.

The people may not have known what was going on inside

the bank, but they could hardly escape noticing that the supply of money in circulation grew from 50 billion cruzeiros in 1948 to 185 billion in 1955. In the latter year, prices rose 40 per cent. And the Socialists persuaded the people that the only way to handle rising prices was to see that wages went up even faster.

The government of Dr. Juscelino Kubitschek, elected in 1955, was dominated by left-wingers, especially "Jango" Goulart, the spokesmen of the labor unions.

The campaign promise of "50 years of progress in five years" was soon forgotten as wages and prices spiraled upward. The government pleaded for — and received — aid from the United States to help it stabilize its money.

More than 1 billion dollars in American aid has been used instead to feed the inflation.

Instead of being stabilized, the cruzeiro slipped down and down. From 20 to the dollar, it fell to 70 in 1957, 170 in 1958, 360 in early 1962; 1,000 in early 1963, and 1,600 last April.

Commercial interest rates rose to 30 per cent but still found few lenders — except for the puppet Bank of Brazil, which continued to lend money at 12 per cent to industrialists on the theory that they would enlarge their plants; instead they poured the money into current inventory in order to make a quick profit. As always happens in such situations, nobody was interested in saving money. The smarter the operator, the quicker he spent it — often abroad.

Unable to cope with the economic problems, Dr. Kubitschek sought to immortalize himself by squandering fantastic sums on a new capital city called Brasilia — which is still unfinished.

The end of Kubitschek's term brought a year of political turmoil approaching civil war, and the end of 1961 found the Socialist Goulart in the presidency. Urgent pleas for restraint from the United States were greeted by assertions that Brazil wasn't going to be forced into "the cold bath" of fiscal austerity. Prices rose 52 per cent in 1962 and doubled in 1963. Private investment from the United States, already discouraged by fear of nationalization, slowed to a trickle. Meanwhile, the Bank of Brazil ran out of gold and suspended payments abroad.

In April, 1964, Goulart was deposed by a military revolt, and a new government was installed which has managed so far — by drastic economies — to hold the cruzeiro steady at about 1,750 to the dollar. It will be years, however, before the average Brazilian, who was protected neither by the labor unions nor the government, can recover from the effects of inflation. Unlike the average Frenchman or Italian, he cannot fall back on a vast social security system whose benefits can be counted on to escalate with prices.

Brazil's story could be applied to Argentina by making a few changes, such as substituting "Eva Peron" for "Jango Goulart." It has been argued that the Latin American troubles stem from dependence on a one-crop (or one-mineral, as in Chile) economy, with undependable prices. Like war, they undoubtedly contribute to the problem. But other Latin American countries like El Salvador have managed to get along with relatively little inflation. And one country which is beginning to worry about inflation is Sweden, which has a well diversified economy and a long history of peace. But it does have an unbalanced budget brought about largely by welfare expenses. In short, there are many conditions which can play into the hands of inflation; but it has never conquered a country without the collaboration of an extravagant government.

(Editor's Note) Some fourteen years after the above *Chicago Tribune* article, the ravages of extreme inflation continue in Brazil, setting a modern record for duration short of total collapse — but not without horrendous costs in strife, disorder, and impoverishment to the Brazilian victims. Some of these costs are summed up in a recent news article from *Barron's* Financial Weekly:

"Can one 'live with' inflation? The Brazilian government has long answered yes, but some 10,000 auto workers near Sao Paulo last week said no. Wildcat strikes at the Saab-Scania, Ford and Mercedes-Benz plants, in what constitutes the largest industrial region in Latin America, hold both political and economic significance. Last week's walkouts — strictly illegal under Brazilian law — appear to be the most important labor moves in Brazil since 1968, when troops were called in to put down strikers at Osasco, an industrial suburb of Sao Paulo. Brazilian inflation is unremitting, but the authorities, abetted by distinguished economists, have preferred it to the bitter pill of deflation. By official (and disputed) reckoning, the cost of living in Sao Paulo rose 40 percent last year, 38 percent in 1976 and 27 percent in 1975. Long-term contracts of all kinds are 'indexed' for rising prices; minimum wages are adjusted from time to time — by 41 percent on May 1. . . .

"Urban labor unrest lately has mounted. 'The strike,' wrote a *Financial Times* correspondent the other day from Sao Paulo of the walkout at Saab-Scania, 'is indicative of growing discontent among the 100,000 metal workers in the Brazilian automobile industry.' Trade unions argue that their real wages have actually fallen in the past 10 years, a surprising charge in view of the Brazilian 'economic miracle,' which, according to estimates by the U.S. Agency for International Development, has boosted per-capita GNP from $590 in 1970 to $1,400 in 1977. Strikers, in any case, are demanding an immediate 20 percent boost in wages to restore the value of their pay."

Lesson Seven: The Mechanics of the Dollar's Destruction*

WASHINGTON — In a heavily guarded pressroom at the Bureau of Engraving and Printing here, foreman Arthur Baron stands almost surrounded by tangible evidence of a great economic abstraction: the national debt.

Around him stand more than a dozen waist-high stacks of half-printed Treasury bills — government IOUs in the making. Each tightly bound pile consists of 5,000 large sheets of square paper, on which are printed six bills to be valued at $10,000 apiece. Every stack represents $300 million but just looks like an oversize bundle of crisp stationery.

"Those machines over there," says Mr. Baron, pointing to two whirring presses, "used to be printing currency, but now we have them working pretty steadily on the debt."

The fact that Mr. Baron's presses have switched from printing money to printing U.S. debt securities is a telling sign of the times. The federal government, short of money, is long on debt these days. Its money machines are cranking out millions upon millions of these pretty pieces of paper — purple, blue and green and bearing engraved likenesses of long-forgotten Treasury Secretaries and bearded Presidents. . . .

Government borrowing in the fiscal year that began last July 1 is expected to top $80 billion, up from $51 billion in the past year, fiscal 1975, and from just $3 billion in fiscal 1974. At the beginning of the current fiscal year, the federal debt already totalled $544 billion, up 68 percent in a decade. Just paying interest on the debt now costs $36 billion a year, which makes that the government's third most expensive activity, right behind social-welfare spending and national defense. . . .

Treasury officials are trying hard to reduce the ill effects of their borrowing, but the government's huge cash needs leave little room for maneuvering. And at the Federal Reserve Board, there is little inclination to fully accommodate the

*Excerpted from an article in the *Wall Street Journal*, September 30, 1975 by James P. Gannon.

Treasury's needs by pumping up the nation's money supply; the Fed fears that such a course would only feed inflation. . . .

Treasury debt managers, trying to dream up ways to borrow more than $80 billion this fiscal year, are trapped between the rock of the Fed and the hard place of their own cash needs. "You have nothing but bad choices," comments Edward Snyder, a veteran Treasury debt-management specialist, who likens the present situation to the borrowing binge needed to finance World War II.

Under these circumstances, the Treasury must constantly, rather than occasionally, tap the credit market. Sales of intermediate and long-term issues — notes and bonds — are being scheduled two and three times a month, usually in bites of $1 billion to $3 billion, instead of quarterly as before. Weekly auctions of three-month and six-month Treasury bills are raising $700 million to $1 billion of "new money" — money beyond that needed to pay off maturing bills.

"We're operating in a fundamentally different climate from that in which the Treasury has operated in the past," contends Edwin H. Yeo III, the former Pittsburgh bank economist who became under secretary for monetary affairs — chief debt-juggler — two months ago. Not only are the Treasury's needs much bigger, Mr. Yeo says, but financial markets are "more volatile" — subject to wider and more frequent ups and downs as inflation fears and other psychological factors dictate.

The Treasury is adjusting its financial operation to this jittery climate in different ways, the official suggests. One effort is minute-by-minute monitoring of bond-and-stock-market activity. . . .

Besides watching the market more, Treasury men are trying to tell the market more about their financing plans. They recently outlined in public their elaborate plan for raising $44 billion to $47 billion in new money during the current July-December period. Why? "Our feeling was that the markets were uncertain about our plans, and uncertainty is anathema to markets," Mr. Yeo remarks. By letting dealers and investors know well in advance the amounts and types of coming Treasury debt issues, Mr. Yeo hopes to calm some of the jitters that can result in wide price swings and interest-rate changes.

Only half in jest, debt manager Ed Snyder sums up the Treasury's problem: "Debt management today is easy. There aren't too many choices to make. You just do all of everything that you can think of and hope that it is enough."

How the Fed Intervenes in Currency Markets*

NEW YORK — Every now and then, the foreign-exchange trading room of a big bank here will get a phone call from a middle-sized Midwestern bank that wants to buy dollars in return for German marks. In the hubbub of a market handling $5 billion daily, the order attracts little attention.

The Midwest bank perhaps is acting on behalf of a local manufacturer. The company might have just sold tractors to a German importer and wants to exchange the marks it received for dollars it needs to meet its payroll.

Generally, that's exactly what's going on. But sometimes it isn't. Sometimes an obscure, poker-faced bank is playing a quite different part. Such a bank may be cast in the unlikely role of a secret agent in the Carter administration's battle to defend the dollar; the bank may be carrying out confidential orders received directly from the operations center in the New York Federal Reserve Bank. . . .

Whether the Fed's methods and resources are adequate is still to be fully tested. "Although order has been restored to the market, it remains to be seen" whether expectations about U.S. inflation have changed enough to "put an end to nearly a year and a half of dollar weakness," Chase Manhattan Bank cautions. Unless opinion abroad turns more favorable, "the expenditure of the entire $30 billion defense fund might not suffice," observes Donaldson, Lufkin & Jenrette, a New York securities firm. . . .

The Fed's so-called intervention is its major day-to-day means of keeping the dollar safely away from its recent brink

*Excerpted from an article in the *Wall Street Journal* of November 14, 1978 by Richard F. Janssen.

of panic. Much of the time, the Fed tries to remain undetected in its marketplace forays. If it can create the impression of a "natural" increase in demand for dollars, it may give pause to traders poised to unload dollars.

Using an obscure outlying bank as its secret agent can be effective in such covert activity — provided the market is quiet. Obviously, a middlesized bank can buy just so many dollars without attracting attention. And such modest purchases can affect the price of the dollar only when trading is slow.

On busier days, the Fed often turns to trusted traders at some of the biggest New York banks. As long as the traders keep mum, even Fed orders for hundreds of millions of dollars can be blended in with these banks' regular business without disclosing an artificial tinge to the wave of demand. (Many dealers around the world contend, however, that they can always tell when the Fed is intervening.). . .

Because the Fed has become more activist, the relationship between it and traders has become increasingly "adversary." But they apparently agree that the Fed quite possibly will be intervening heavily in coming weeks and months.

Bibliography

Anderson, B.A., *Economics and the Public Welfare*, D. Van Nostrand and Company, Inc., Princeton, N.J., 1949

Angell, Norman, *The Story of Money*, Frederick A. Stokes Co., New York, 1929

Bakewell, Paul, Jr. *Inflation in the United States*, The Caxton Printers, Ltd., Caldwell, Idaho, 1962

———, *What Are We Using For Money*, D. Van Nostrand and Company, Inc., New York, N.Y., 1952

Bastiat, Frederic, *Economic Harmonies*, The Foundation for Economic Education, Inc., Irvington-on-Hudson, N.Y., 1964

———, *Economic Sophisms*, The Foundation for Economic Education, Inc., Irvington-on-Hudson, N.Y. 1964

———, *The Law*, The Foundation for Economic Education, Inc., Irvington-on-Hudson, N.Y., 1956

———, *Selected Essays on Political Economy*, The Foundation for Economic Education, Inc., Irvington-on-Hudson, N.Y., 1964

de la Boetie, Etienne, *The Politics of Obedience: A Discourse on Voluntary Servitude*, Free Life Editions, New York, 1975

Böhm-Bawerk, E., *Capital and Interest*, Libertarian Press, South Holland, Illinois, 1959

Bradford, Frederick A., *Money and Banking*, Longmans, Green and Co., New York, 1934

Bronowski, J. and Mazlish Bruce, *The Western Intellectual Tradition*, Hutchinson & Co. Ltd., London, 1960

Butts, Allison, Editor, and Charles D. Coxe, *Silver: Economics, Metallurgy and Use*, D. Van Nostrand, Princeton, N.J., 1967

Caldwell, Taylor, *Captains and the Kings*, Fawcett Publications, Inc., Greenwich, Connecticut, 1972

Commodity Research Bureau, Editors, *Commodity Yearbook*, Commodity Research Bureau, Inc., New York

Dampier, Sir William Cecil, *A History of Science*, Cambridge At the University Press, New York, 1961

Dunbar, Charles F., *The Theory and History of Banking*, G.P. Putnam's Sons, New York, 1922

Fehrenbach, T.R., *The Swiss Banks*, McGraw Hill, N.Y., 1966

Groseclose, Elgin, *Money and Man*, Ungar, New York, 1961

_____, *The Decay of Money*, Institute for Monetary Research, Inc., Washington, D.C., 1962

Handy & Harman, *The Silver Market in 19--*, (Annual), Handy & Harman, New York

Harper, F.A., *Liberty — A Path to its Recovery*, The Foundation for Economic Education, Irvington-on-Hudson, New York, 1949

Hayek, F.A., *Denationalisation of Money*, The Institute of Economic Affairs, London, 1976

_____, *Monetary Theory and the Trade Cycle*, Augustus M. Kelley, Clifton, N.J., 1975

_____, *Prices and Production*, Augustus M. Kelley, New York, 1967

_____, *The Road to Serfdom*, The University of Chicago Press, Chicago, Illinois, 1962

Hazlitt, Henry, *The Critics of Keynesian Economics*, D. Van Nostrand Company, Inc., Princeton, N.J., 1960

_____, *Economics in One Lesson*, Pocket Books, Inc., New York, 1948

_____, *What You Should Know About Inflation*, D. Van Nostrand Company, Inc., Princeton, N.J., 1965

Homer, Sidney, *A History of Interest Rates*, Rutgers University Press, New Brunswick, N.J., 1963

Hutton, Graham, *What Killed Prosperity*, Chilton Company, New York, 1961

International Monetary Fund, Editors, *Finance & Development*, Washington, D.C. (Annual)

Kuhn, Thomas S., *The Structure of Scientific Revolutions*, The University of Chicago Press, Chicago, Illinois, 1975

Leoni, Bruno, *Freedom and the Law*, D. Van Nostrand Company, Inc., Princeton, N.J., 1961

Lerner, E., *Inflation in the Confederacy, 1861-1865*, University of Chicago

McKay, Charles, *Extraordinary Popular Delusions and the Madness of Crowds*, L.C. Page & Co., Boston, Mass., 1932

Mitchell, W., *Gold, Prices, & Wages Under the Greenback Standard*, U.S. Congress, Joint Economic Committee Report

Morgan, E. Victor, *A History of Money*, Penguin Books, Baltimore, Maryland, 1965

Paris, Alexander P., *The Coming Credit Collapse*, Arlington House Publishers, Westport, Conn., 1980

Popper, Karl R., *The Open Society and Its Enemies*, Princeton University Press, Princeton, N.J., 1966

Pugsley, John A., *The Alpha Strategy*, The Common Sense Press, Inc., Costa Mesa, California, 1980

———, *Common Sense Economics*, The Common Sense Press, Inc., Costa Mesa, California, 1976

Rand, Ayn, *Atlas Shrugged*, Random House, New York, 1957

———, *The Fountainhead*, Bobbs Merrill, New York, 1947

Rickenbacker, William F., *The Twelve-Year Sentence*, Open Court Publishing Company, 1974

Riegel, E.C., *Private Enterprise Money*, Harbinger House, New York, 1944

Röpke, Wilhelm, *A Humane Economy*, Henry Regnery Company, Chicago, Illinois, 1971

Rothbard, Murray N., *America's Great Depression*, D. Van Nostrand Company, Inc., Princeton, N.J., 1963

———, *For A New Liberty*, The Macmillan Company, New York, 1973

———, *Man, Economy, and State*, (Vol. I & II), D. Van Nostrand Company, Inc., Princeton, N.J.,1962

———, *Power and Market — Government and the Economy*, Institute for Humane Studies, Inc., Menlo Park, California, 1970

———, *What Has Government Done to Our Money?*, Pine Tree Press, Colorado Springs, Colorado, 1963

Rueff, Jacques, *The Age of Inflation*, Regnery, 1964

———, *The Monetary Sin of the West*, The Macmillan Company, New York, 1972

Smith, Adam, *The Wealth of Nations*, The Modern Library, New York, 1965

Studenski, Paul, and Krooss, H.E., *Financial History of the United States*, McGraw, 1963

Sumner, W., *History of American Currency*, Henry Holt, New York, 1874

Thoreau, Henry David, *Walden or Life in the Woods; On the Duty of Civil Disobedience*, The New American Library, New York, 1960

Veatch, Henry B., *Aristotle — A Contemporary Appreciation*, Indiana University Press, Bloomingdale, Indiana, 1974

Von Mises, Ludwig, *Human Action*, William Hodge and Company Limited, London, 1949

———, *Omnipotent Government: The Rise of the Total State and Total War*, Arlington House, New Rochelle, N.Y., 1969

———, *Socialism*, Jonathan Cape, London, 1972

————, *Theory and History*, Yale University Press, New Haven, 1957

————, *The Theory of Money and Credit*, Yale University Press, New Haven, Conn., 1953

White, A., *Fiat Money Inflation in France*, The Caxton Printers, Ltd., Caldwell, Idaho, 1958

Woodward, W.E., *A New American History*, Garden City Publishing Co., Inc., Garden City, N.Y., 1938

————, *Tom Paine America's Godfather*, E.P. Dutton & Company , Inc., New York, 1945

Index

197